What people are saying about

Breaking Through the Silicon Ceiling

Chris King is one of a kind. Her singular focus on the customer and business outcomes was a lesson to all of us growing up at IBM. She was a role model for me as the first female CEO in the semiconductor industry and has such an inspiring story of how she got there.
Lisa Su, President & CEO of AMD

While this is the story of an amazing woman's life and career, there are many very important lessons here for *all* of us.
John E. Kelly III, IBM Executive Vice President—retired, and tech industry veteran

Chris King's life and career is a remarkable story of triumph over adversity, proving yet again that nothing is impossible if you are smart, determined, and willing to look beyond whatever obstacles come your way. This remarkable book is an inspiration for anyone looking to make a better life.
Stanley M. Bergman, CEO of Henry Schein

Breaking Through the Silicon Ceiling

How a 20-year-old Single Mother
Became the World's First Female
Semiconductor Company CEO

Breaking Through the Silicon Ceiling

How a 20-year-old Single Mother
Became the World's First Female
Semiconductor Company CEO

Christine King

Gerald Lee Kimber White

BUSINESS
BOOKS

London, UK
Washington, DC, USA

CollectiveInk

First published by Business Books, 2024
Business Books is an imprint of Collective Ink Ltd.,
Unit 11, Shepperton House, 89 Shepperton Road, London, N1 3DF
office@collectiveink.com
www.collectiveink.com
www.collectiveink.com/business-books

For distributor details and how to order please visit the 'Ordering' section on our website.

Text copyright: Christine King 2023

ISBN: 978 1 80341 505 5
978 1 80341 506 2 (ebook)
Library of Congress Control Number: 2023933873

A CIP catalogue record for this book is available from the British Library.

Design: Lapiz Digital Services

UK: Printed and bound by CPI Group (UK) Ltd, Croydon, CR0 4YY
Printed in North America by CPI GPS partners

We operate a distinctive and ethical publishing philosophy in all areas of our business, from our global network of authors to production and worldwide distribution.

Contents

To my lab partner — then, now, and always

C.K.

Preface

April 1970

Ding, the gas pump chimed, as if to remind me that I was pouring my last pennies into the tank. I had 66 cents to my name, and I was using every one of them to buy two gallons of gas. My always active toddler, Eric, was squirming in the back seat, anxious for me to finish and for us to get back on the road home. "Keep your feet on the seat," I called through the window, worried that his foot would punch through the rusted floorboard of my Mustang.

It had been a long day of searching for a job. I was bone-weary and leaned on the car for a moment of respite. I closed my eyes to shield them from the glare of the station's lights and reflected on the events of the day; just one more in a week of days spent fruitlessly reviewing classified ads and making the rounds of local businesses trying to find a job that could support our family. Well, Eric and me. My husband had left us a week ago. He had always been a free spirit, so I guess I shouldn't have been too surprised when he came home one evening and said he was leaving. "It's nothing personal. I just don't want to be married," he explained. That may have been so, but it felt kind of personal to me. We hadn't been married long, but we had a family, and now he had left Eric and me to fend for ourselves.

Eric and I lived in a rundown trailer park with the stereotypical cast of characters — drunks, lechers, abusers, and folks like us who were good people, just poor and trying to get by. Over the past week, I had been looking for a job — *any* job — to fix the increasingly desperate situation we were in, but I quickly discovered I was starting with three strikes against me. I was a woman, with all that meant in the 1970s. One company said they wanted to offer me a clerical job, but they couldn't because I was "too pretty" and would distract the men on the factory floor. Second, I was a 20-year-old single mom. I recalled the interview earlier in the day at a bank that couldn't hire me to be a teller because they "couldn't count on me to show up for my work shift if my son got sick." My third strike was my lack of education; I only had a high school diploma. I was just one of millions of unemployed, minimally skilled people in the middle of what was called a "mild recession." Again, it didn't feel mild to me as I was turned down for job after job.

Ding.

That was it. Literally all of my money was gone, and I had no idea how, where, or when I would get more. I sighed, replaced the pump nozzle, got back into the car, and slumped down in the driver's seat. I had two gallons of gas, a few odds and ends in the pantry at home, and a future that felt bleak and out of control. I alternated between passive hopelessness and active frustration that every option and every path forward seemed closed off to me. Fear began to well up inside at the thought of our dire circumstances, but Eric's cheerful squeaks and noises from the back seat reminded me that self-pity was a luxury that I couldn't afford.

As I sat there for a moment to collect myself, Bob Dylan's "All Along the Watchtower" lyrics came to mind, "There must be some way out of here." *Man, I wish*, I thought ruefully to myself as I reached forward to turn the key. The car roared to life like a wind beginning to howl, and though I didn't know it as I pulled out of the station, I was about to discover my way out of there.

Introduction

August 2015

"Now what?" The members of QLogic's Board of Directors were slumped in their chairs around the boardroom table, sitting silently and looking gravely at each other in the company's California headquarters.

The task before us was unpleasant and the path forward unclear. We had a big decision to make. QLogic's Chief Executive Officer (CEO) was failing and we had to do something. This was actually the second CEO in a row to fail to reverse the company's revenue decline, and things were getting desperate. We felt the weight of our investors' expectations on our shoulders, not to mention the livelihoods and futures of our employees.

Several of us on the board had been CEOs in the past. We all knew it was a challenging job and that leading turnarounds made the job even more difficult. No one on QLogic's executive team was ready to step up into the role, and recruiting a CEO from outside the company would take too long and risk a third failure. So, we knew it was up to one of us to take over and lead the company forward. The atmosphere in the room was tense and subdued. Everyone was pensive, with no one knowing or wanting to suggest a potential path forward. Everyone was looking at each other; no one wanted to volunteer to lead or say anything.

Suddenly, Scott, one of my fellow board members and always the one to speak up first, turned to me. "Chris, you know you're the best person to fix this. What do you say? Would you consider taking the reins as Executive Chairman?"

The room quickly nodded in agreement as they looked hopefully toward me. I was humbled by the recommendation and the room's confidence in me, but I was also a little wary (or maybe weary!). I thought to myself, *I've already retired twice as*

CEO after taking one company public and turning around another. Do I want to sign up for another 24/7 gig? But I find tackling difficult problems that I can solve irresistible. Maybe Scott knew this when he asked.

The challenge before us *was* significant. QLogic had been a successful, growing company for 20 years, providing the networking gear underpinning the digital revolution sweeping the world. Success can be a sleeping pill, though, and the company had not kept up with the times. In recent years its revenue growth had stalled and now its future was in real jeopardy. I weighed the challenge of the situation against the assets I would have to help me turn the company around, namely a good board and leadership team that included a great Chief Financial Officer (CFO).

"Yes, let's do this," I finally responded, without a clear vision of *how* we would do it. What I *did* have was the confidence that we would figure it out. After all, "figuring it out" had become one of my specialties over the course of going from being an uneducated 20-year-old single mother, to becoming the world's first female CEO of a semiconductor company, to now sitting on the boards of several global technology leaders. We would figure it out.

October 2023

I decided to write this book because we are living through an era where the gap between the "haves" and the "have-nots" is widening. For some, that gap is beginning to feel like an uncrossable chasm, where success is only possible if you already have the financial resources and connections that come from privilege. You could be excused for thinking that being born with a silver spoon in your mouth is a prerequisite for social and economic progress when you look at today's typical business, entertainment, and political leaders and consider the hurdles to reaching that level. As someone who came from a blue-collar background without a penny to my name or any relationships I could leverage, however, I can assure you that your future success is not defined by your origin. Even today.

Obviously, starting a few steps up the ladder is a big advantage, but the seeds of real success lie *within you* and are available to *everyone*. In fact, in my experience, adversity is an essential ingredient to future success because it forces us to learn, change, and grow to become more than we were before. It broadens our perspective and pushes us to explore and navigate new paths. It isn't easy, but it strengthens and prepares us for what is to come. The most successful people I know—from both professional and personal perspectives—have regularly struggled over the course of their lives.

In this book, I share 12 lessons I have learned over the course of my life and career, which taken together serve as a blueprint for the success I have found time and time again across wildly divergent professional fields—from technology, to healthcare, to utilities, and even dairy farming and equestrian competition! These lessons apply at all stages of your career—from entry level to retirement (and even beyond). My path has certainly not been straightforward or always clear as I was going through it, but I have found professional success and, most importantly, profound personal satisfaction along the way.

My hope, dear reader, is that you see yourself in these stories and are inspired to dream your biggest dreams and do the hard work to turn those dreams into your reality. And remember to have fun along the way!

Chris King

Chapter 1

The Dawn (1970–1973)

As I drove my son Eric home on an April evening in 1970 after another frustrating day of searching for a job, the signs of spring were all around me, but I felt trapped in an unrelentingly harsh and dark winter. I was running into obstacles no matter which way I turned. My husband had left us. I couldn't find a job. My family and friends couldn't or wouldn't help me. I was completely out of money and hope. Well, not completely out of hope. I knew that I could still make something of myself and support my son if someone would just give me a chance. Right now, though, no one was lining up to help me out.

Driving down the dark highway, I thought wistfully to myself, *I wish I could just start over fresh with a blank slate.* Growing up in a blue-collar, post-war family, though, I knew you couldn't just wipe your slate clean and start over. My mom was a housewife (and aspiring artist) and my dad ran a very small business he inherited from his father-in-law fixing kitchen stoves. They weren't particularly fond of my unwise decision to marry John, a hippie who looked great and played a mean guitar, but who only had a sixth-grade education. That decision had landed me outside my family's good graces in more ways than one. No, my slate had 20 years' worth of notes, calculations, and doodles on it, and I could no more erase them and start over than I could erase the fact that I was now a poor single mom with extremely limited prospects.

I didn't realize it at the time, but there are benefits to not having a blank slate. I would learn that our past experiences— good or bad—give us knowledge, wisdom, and the tools we need to build our future. I have learned to approach what can be viewed negatively as past "baggage" as a resource. Our joys and sorrows, our triumphs and failures, represent a toolbox out of which we can build a better tomorrow.

Of course, at the time, all I could see was a cluttered slate, with no room to begin to write a better future for Eric or myself. When we got home, I was feeling depressed and even Eric's antics weren't of interest. I looked wearily around the cheap, dreary trailer and thought, *This stinks. I have to figure out SOME way to get us out of here and start building a real future.*

The Dawn (1970–1973)

It was at that moment that my eyes came to rest on the textbooks from the two community college courses I had taken for fun after high school. I had taken night classes in psychology and Western civilization simply because I liked learning new things and they were subjects that interested me. Those books had been gathering dust on my makeshift bookshelf ever since, but tonight, as I reflected on the day's fruitless job search, pouring the last of my money into my car's tank at the gas station, and my overall desperate circumstances, they almost seemed to glow with possibility and potential.

The application forms I filled out during my job search had all asked if I had a college degree. They weren't interested in someone who was a college "tourist" who had taken a couple of courses for fun. They wanted candidates with the intellectual capacity and discipline to pursue a full course of study to completion. They wanted people who brought a strong base of knowledge and expertise to their jobs.

It became crystal clear to me that *without education, knowledge, or skills, I was nowhere.* I had no differentiators, nothing of real value to offer potential employers, and as a result, I had gotten nowhere. Without an education, that wasn't going to change. *So that's the solution then,* I said to myself. *The only way out of this is to go to college full-time and get a degree.* I knew it wouldn't be easy, but honestly, what did I have to lose? I had to at least try.

But how to get started? There was no one I could ask about how to get a college degree—none of my family or friends had ever attended college. And I certainly didn't have the money for college. Beyond that, taking care of Eric was a full-time job. The obstacles to getting a degree felt insurmountable. It occurred to me, though, that maybe one of my former professors would remember me and be able to give me some advice. I didn't know if they could help me, but they were the best shot I had. As far as I could see, they were the *only* shot I had.

So, the next day, I loaded Eric into the Mustang and drove to nearby Orange County Community College (OCCC) in Middletown, New York, to speak with my psychology professor, Mr. White. We sat in his dim, cramped office lined with overflowing bookshelves. Eric played on the floor while I laid out my situation. I told him that John had left me the week before and I didn't know where he was. I told him that I was completely on my own. I told him that I had put the last of my money into the gas tank the night before and at this point I didn't know where our next dollar would come from. I told him about the obstacles I had run into while trying to find a job and that the only real option I had was to get a college degree that would make me a more viable job candidate.

When I finished my litany of woes, I expected him to applaud my decision to get a college education and build a future for myself, but it quickly became clear that he wasn't thinking about my future. He was thinking about my present.

"College?" he asked incredulously. "You have no money. You shouldn't be worrying about your education right now. You should be worrying about how you're going to *live*."

After an initial moment of shock and deflation, I almost burst into tears. I didn't need someone to tell me that my son and I were on the edge of disaster. I already knew that. I needed someone to tell me how to fix it!

Mr. White scribbled down the contact information for our local social services center on a scrap of paper and handed it to me with the direction to seek their help to get the money I needed to live. Our conversation was over. It wasn't the aspirational, inspirational, or emotional conversation about my future that I had envisioned. It was a brief, transactional, problem-solving session, and while I was disappointed to walk away with that college degree no closer than it was before our meeting, I knew he had at least given me a lifeline on the slip of paper I clutched in my hands.

Coming from a working-class family in that era, I had never considered social services and welfare as a possibility. It wasn't an issue of pride. I just didn't know I could get free money from someone. That sounded great to me! I drove straight to the social services department, and after completing the paperwork and a subsequent visit from the social worker assigned to my case, I was granted a monthly stipend and food stamps.

I'm sure the social worker was just checking the boxes during her visit to our trailer, but I took advantage of her presence and knowledge to share my vision of enrolling in college full-time. She looked up from her clipboard skeptically and said, "Well, that's interesting," in a tone that indicated that my goal wasn't very likely. The cost of college aside, her biggest concern was what I was going to do with Eric while I was in classes. She had a point. I couldn't lug him to my classes every day. I needed to figure that out.

The next day, I started exploring daycare possibilities for Eric, and one in particular stood out for me. The price was right—only $4 a day—but what I most liked was that they seemed to care about what made Eric tick. They asked what his favorite TV show was (*Lost in Space*) and if he had a favorite song ("American Pie" by Don McLean). *This is the place*, I thought to myself.

I went home that evening and sat at the kitchen table working out a schedule and budget that would allow me to put Eric in daycare and take classes four days a week without breaking the bank. It wasn't pretty, but it would work. Of course, selling my social worker on my vision was not going to be easy. That monthly stipend was meant to pay for living expenses, not luxuries like a college education. But in my mind, college wasn't a luxury; it was a necessity. It was the only thing I could think of that would allow me to finally get a job and support my family.

I continued working on my sales pitch into the night. I tied my education to a goal she could appreciate—getting me off welfare. I laid out a course of study that would end with my earning a teaching certificate. Teaching was basically a guaranteed, well-paying job, and it was the most logical path to self-sufficiency. But having a good goal wasn't enough to "make the sale," so I considered all the angles, the pros and cons of my plan, and the objections she might have, developing responses for each of them. Finally, I felt ready to present my idea to the social worker.

A couple of days later, I made my pitch. She did raise many of the concerns I had thought of, but ultimately, she begrudgingly replied, "If you can make it work financially, I won't stop you, but we can't give you any more money. If you get yourself into trouble, it's on you."

Despite her tepid response, I was on top of the world! I was so proud of the fact that I had been able to convince her to give me the chance. I'm sure I was beaming. In that moment, I wanted to give myself a high five for what I considered a huge victory. I had made the sale, and I was going to college!

The next day, I dropped Eric off at his new daycare and went to the administration office at OCCC to enroll as a full-time student. After completing the paperwork, they handed me a bill of $200 for the semester. That was a lot of money for me, but I wasn't worried. Tuition wasn't due until September, and if I earned good grades the State of New York would reimburse me $100. This was absolutely doable if I saved my money and worked hard.

The next decision was the subject I would major in on the way to my teaching certificate. As I considered my options, I remembered how much I had enjoyed my Western civilization class at OCCC. It was the first time that someone had brought history to life for me, giving me a larger perspective on the world and my place in it. I decided that learning and teaching history would be interesting, and when I discovered that OCCC didn't offer an education degree, I signed up for the next best thing—an associate's degree in the arts with a major in social sciences.

After a summer of saving my pennies and rebuilding a life for Eric and myself, I matriculated in the fall of 1970 with a full slate of classes—English, math, creative writing, and astronomy. When I had taken my earlier night classes, I had heard from the other students which professors were the best ones at the school. The quirky ones seemed to be the most popular and I heard that one of them in particular, the astronomy professor Dr. Gard, was one of the best and smartest professors at OCCC. I always liked looking up at the stars, so I figured *Why not?* and signed up for his class.

When I got to the first class, Dr. Gard looked like the stereotypical absent-minded professor with a big gray beard, Einstein-esque hair, and glasses, and he topped off the look by riding a bike to his classes. In that first class, Dr. Gard launched straight into talking about the beginning of the universe and how small we are in the whole scheme of things. It was an eye-opening and thoroughly engaging class.

As time went on, I realized Dr. Gard was maybe the smartest person I had ever known. He had earned a PhD in chemistry before World War Two. When the US entered the war and he was drafted, he registered as a conscientious objector. As a result, he was assigned to a difficult detail in the South Pacific, where he contracted malaria and other tropical diseases. After the atomic bomb was dropped on Hiroshima, the Army sent Dr. Gard into the city with the first troops as a medic due to his extensive knowledge of chemistry. It was such a horrific situation and experience for Dr. Gard that he decided he would subsequently focus on astronomy because "it was so far out there, no one could do any harm with it."

While in Hiroshima, Dr. Gard happened to come across a film crew that had been shooting a movie before the bomb. They had switched their focus to make the only "on the ground" movie of what had happened. The film was banned in the US for years after the war, but Dr. Gard had a personal copy. When I became the president of the Engineering and Technology Society at OCCC, we showed that film to our group, which they continued to do every year after that (I hope they still do!). It was extremely hard to watch, but very necessary.

One thing that struck me over the course of that first semester with Dr. Gard was that he never took roll call or called any of the students by name. I also noticed that some of the students took advantage of that and didn't show up to class much. I was shocked when I learned that they had failed the class due to lack of participation. How did Dr. Gard know who was and wasn't in a class of more than 70 people when he never seemed to take a roll call? I asked him about that, and he said that everyone tends to have their name on something, like their bags or books, and he could read upside down, so he had logged the slackers in his mind while he walked around the class during his lectures!

My classes that first semester weren't easy and exercised mental muscles and discipline that I hadn't used in a while, but I worked hard and managed to end the semester with all A grades except for a B in that darn creative-writing class.

I had gotten an A+ in astronomy and enjoyed it so much that I decided to take another semester with Dr. Gard in the spring. One day, I happened to notice Dr. Gard going into a small room outside the lecture hall. The door was open, so I peeked in and saw him sitting at some sort of computer terminal. Dr. Gard could be intimidating and I was intruding on his work, but I felt brave enough to clear my throat, apologize for the interruption, and ask him what he was doing. He looked up from what I would learn was a Model 33 teletype terminal and told me he was hooked into the Dartmouth time-sharing system and writing computer programs. I had never seen such a thing and thought to myself, *Wow! That is pretty cool!*

In the very early 1970s, that was amazing and, for the first time, I was introduced to and began to understand the power of technology.

As I ended my second semester with Dr. Gard, and earned another A+, I told him that I was going to take classes from the electrical engineering technology curriculum in the fall. I only needed one more semester of courses to get my associate's degree, and the best part was I only needed electives so I could study anything I wanted. He looked at me with equal parts surprise, pride, and inspiration, and then shocked me by offering me a job as his technical assistant. The college had received funding to build a small observatory and Dr. Gard was focused on the electronics at the base of a telescope. He said that I could start immediately and work all summer before school started in the fall. The pay was good and amounted to as much as I was getting from welfare. I was so excited as I called my case worker the very next day and told her I had gotten a job and didn't need my welfare check anymore. I was amused when I subsequently discovered the power of bureaucracy and that the checks kept coming. It took me dozens of calls and messages to get off welfare. It actually took me longer to get off of welfare than it had taken for me to get on it!

I loved my astronomy classes and working with Dr. Gard on the telescope's electronics, but the real reason I wanted to take electrical engineering courses wasn't his influence; it was romance. I did it to impress a guy.

Before my OCCC journey began, when John and I were still married, we had met Terry King, the chief engineer at the local radio station, WALL, and a bit of a local hero. My husband John was a talented jack-of-all-trades and had bounced around a number of jobs—from carpentry to metal machining to shoeing horses. One evening, John was headed to shoe a horse and asked me if I wanted to come along, so I loaded up Eric and off we went.

As it turned out, Terry and Judy King were horse sitting for John's horseshoe client while he was away on vacation. When John finished shoeing the horse, Terry invited us into their house and the four of us ended up hitting it off, swapping stories and discussing everything from photography to our kids. John spied a guitar leaning against the wall and picked it up and started playing Creedence Clearwater Revival's "Proud Mary." John's great voice and guitar strumming filled the room and Terry and Judy were duly impressed by this guy who could shoe horses and was an outstanding musician to boot. Terry, who was a fix-it guy, and John, a horse of many colors, formed a friendship in that moment and started hanging out together.

Six months later, when John informed me he didn't want to be married anymore, I was stunned. I didn't know what to do or where to go, so I called Judy. She and Terry felt horrible about the situation and invited me to come over. When I got there, Eric was sleeping in my arms and Judy took me upstairs where she had a crib all ready for Eric. I was so grateful to have friends to help me through that terrible night and the days and weeks to come.

I didn't know it at the time, but Terry and Judy were in the midst of divorcing as well, and as Terry and I spent more time together, jointly caring for our children as we went through our own individual hells over the next few months, we started to become attracted to each other. Terry was really into electronics — his basement was full of electronic parts, catalogues of the latest components, soldering irons, and tools. It wasn't just a job for him; it was his passion. He spent hours in his basement building and tinkering with electronic devices. It all looked intriguing to me, and I thought I could make myself even more interesting to Terry — and better compete with the other women out there — if I learned something about electronics and engineering.

I had accumulated the credits I needed for my major from my first year and earlier night classes, so I could graduate in just one more semester taking only electives. OCCC had an electrical engineering technology curriculum, and since I could study anything I wanted, I decided to go all in, signing up for electronics, physics, computer programming, and calculus.

Before the classes started, I went to the college bookstore to purchase the textbooks I needed. When I took the books home and opened them, though, I was astounded. It looked like Greek to me. I thought to myself, *What have I gotten myself into?!* I hadn't taken much science in high school, and I wasn't very successful at the little I took. Looking at page after page of Greek letters and math equations without numbers, I thought nervously to myself, *There is no way I will be able to do this*, and I was amused at how my impetuosity had once again led me to perhaps bite off more than I could chew. Time would tell.

I knew I would be the only woman in my classes that fall, but I wasn't nervous about that. I actually couldn't imagine why other women weren't doing the same thing as me and taking the male-dominated classes I was. Being the only woman in a class full of attractive guys sounded pretty good to me! My primary concern remained whether I could understand this stuff. I was going to need some help.

My very first engineering class in September 1971 was Electronics 101. I decided to find the smartest and best-looking guy in the room to be my lab partner; someone who knew something about this mystery of electronics and could help me decipher the world of technology. The electronics professor started the first class by going around the room and asking each student to introduce themselves and say whether they had any experience in electronics. I was in the front row, so I described my work at the radio station and in the astronomy lab. When they got to the back of the room, a strong, nice-looking guy named Jack said he had worked on radar on

B-52 airplanes in the Air Force. *That's him*, I thought to myself. I figured that with his expertise and experience, he'd be able to show me the ropes in my classes and he looked like someone who would be fun, too! The following Friday was my first lab for the electronics class and Jack was in the same lab class as me! *Perfect*, I thought to myself, and ran up to him to ask if he had a lab partner. When he told me no, I replied, "Well, you have one now!" I think he was taken aback that the only girl in the class had chosen him to be his partner. I probably further bewildered him when I followed up that request by asking if he could give me a ride home, picking up Eric from daycare on the way. My Mustang had stopped working and was rusting away in our yard at that point, so I was hitch-hiking to get everywhere. Jack kindly agreed to both requests and I will never forget what he said as he opened the door for me to get into his gleaming 1969 Chevelle Super Sport, "Wipe your feet." That was Jack and his characteristic fastidiousness and discipline in a nutshell, which would rub off on me over time as we got to know each other as lab partners and, eventually, best friends.

Within the first week of classes, I was pleasantly surprised to find that I had lucked into some great professors, including a young priest who taught physics. I also discovered that the reality of studying technology was better than my initial glance at the textbooks had led me to believe. Over the next couple of months, I found I had a knack for technology. It was certainly easier than the humanities. When a humanities professor grades your creative essay, it's somewhat subjective. In technology and engineering, either you're right or you're wrong. I excelled in a world of such certainty. A new passion for engineering blossomed within me and I began to shift from viewing education as merely a pathway to a job (I had never really been passionate about teaching) and more as something that was fun in and of itself. Little did I know it at the time, but it would also be a pathway to a very lucrative career.

Halfway through that first semester, AT&T was facing a discrimination lawsuit and the local office was combing nearby schools to recruit women with technical backgrounds to work for the company. The OCCC administration told them they only had one woman studying engineering and pointed them in my direction. I only had half of one semester of the engineering curriculum under my belt, but AT&T was in dire straits and they offered me $12,500 a year to drop out and come to work at their New Jersey facility.

I nearly fell out of my seat when they made the offer. It was a huge amount of money, the equivalent of $80–90,000 today! I couldn't believe how much I could make as a technician! But accepting their offer meant that I wouldn't get my college degree, the pursuit of which had become my North Star. I turned AT&T down and I'm sure people thought I was crazy, but if I could make that much as a technician, I thought to myself, imagine how much I could make as an engineer with a degree. When I initially started taking the engineering courses, I had no intention of going beyond that one semester. I just wanted to graduate and get to work, but once AT&T showed me how much more career and financial potential lay in an engineering degree, I went to my academic advisor and told him that I wanted to work on earning a second associate's degree in electrical engineering technology. Over the course of the next two years, during which I immersed myself equally in engineering and campus life, I earned two degrees—an associate's degree in engineering and another one in arts— and I graduated with a 4.0 grade point average (GPA) in the engineering curriculum. After graduation, I married Terry, the man who had inspired me to pursue engineering courses in the first place, and I got my first real job as a senior technician at IBM.

Engineering And Technology Club

CHRIS HARTUNG
FOR
Student Senator

Lesson #1 — Without Skills or an Education, You Are Nowhere

Over the course of my life, I have learned many lessons, and in this book, I will share the 12 lessons that have had the greatest impact on my life. One of the earliest lessons that I learned was that without skills or an education, you are nowhere.

When you were born, you were given the great gift of *potential*. Every child is born with potential; an unearned and truly amazing gift. Your circumstances will shape the pathway to actualizing that potential and determine the ease or difficulty with which you do it. For the lucky few, circumstances can provide a tailwind that makes achieving your full potential easier, but for most people, circumstances are relatively neutral at best, and are headwinds at worst. That said, we have all heard of people (myself included) who overcame the odds of their demographics, socioeconomic status, and even their mistakes to achieve far more success than could have been expected or even hoped for (I would go so far as to argue that sometimes our greatest successes come *because* of those struggles). The secret to success in life is how you navigate and use your circumstances to go from *potentiality* to *reality*.

You see, as wonderful as potential is, it is worthless if you don't transform it into reality. You are one of eight billion people on this planet (as of this writing), all of whom have that same gift of potential, all of whom want to achieve their full potential. If you don't take steps to actualize your potential, you will be undifferentiated from everyone else. You will be nowhere. This lesson slowly sunk in for me as I drove my Mustang around town, applying for and being turned down for job after job from the classified ads. I was competing with who knows how many other candidates, but I brought nothing to the table other than my potential. I was smart, personable, and ambitious, but I hadn't actualized any of that potential yet. And on top of that, my circumstances as a single mom made it hard for others to even *see* my potential!

If you want to be the master of your fate and move beyond your potential, you need a differentiator. In the professional world, that differentiator comes in the form of skills or an education. I didn't know that at the time, but as I looked around my dismal trailer after another fruitless day of looking for jobs, that awareness dawned on me as my eyes landed on my college textbooks; an awareness that quickly crystallized into an irresistible vision for my future.

For me, pursuing an education was the beginning, the catalyst, for an incredibly vibrant and rewarding life. That's not to say that college is the only path to a successful life. It *is* to say that building an area of expertise, a foundation of knowledge and skills that differentiate you from others, is essential. You can be an expert engineer or teacher, but you can also be an expert plumber, truck driver, store manager, or fast-food cook. Whatever you pursue, strive to learn as much as you can and apply it to the best of your ability to actualize your potential and become the best that you can be. Otherwise, you will be just like everyone else.

It is important to remember, though, that gaining skills or getting an education is not a destination; it is a process. We need to continue building our education and competencies over the course of our lives. My education didn't end with my associate's degrees or even later after I obtained my bachelor's degree. My entire life has been a process of exploration in search of new opportunities to learn, whether on the professional side as a manager, salesperson, and executive, or in my personal life as a dairy farmer and cow cutting champion (more about those avocations in future chapters!). To achieve your full potential, you must never stop learning, growing, and improving. It is the only way to success and, frankly, fulfillment in life.

Your path may not be easy, but it is *your* path and it is up to *you* to make the most of it. Whether you're just starting out or well into your career, commit today to building your capabilities. It doesn't even really matter in which area you build it. I started out learning about the humanities in pursuit of a teaching certificate. I ended up switching to engineering, but the expertise I built in both disciplines compounded and gave me skills and differentiation to start in a career that allowed me to continue building my competency and professional value. Even my experience as a dairy farmer gave me insights and skills that I have applied in the non-bovine areas of my life. So, start today and differentiate yourself. Commit to becoming educated and developing skills over the course of your life that make you different from everyone else. Transform your potential into reality.

Lesson #2—When You Have a Vision, Sell It

Vision without action is a daydream. Many people have a vision, some even have great visions, but they lack the discipline to transform that vision into an action plan that can make the vision real. Others may have a vision and even a plan but lack the confidence in their vision or themselves to mention it, sell it to others, and bring it to life. I think that insecurity is one of the tragedies of humanity. How many great ideas have we lost to history because someone didn't have the confidence to bring it into the light?

In my life, I have repeatedly found that the world is receptive to visions and good ideas, especially if they are backed up with a plan. Over the course of my career, I have had to sell my vision numerous times; to my case worker, to my peers, to my managers, to my staff. Many people react negatively to the concept of "selling" people on something, whether a product, service, or idea. But if you genuinely and deeply believe in what you are selling, it becomes a lot easier because you're selling something of purpose and substance, not "fluff."

The first step to selling a vision you believe in is thinking about it from your customer's perspective. When I went to sell my vision of going to college to my caseworker, I had an uphill climb. I didn't know her at all. She wasn't a friend, colleague, or even an acquaintance. I couldn't leverage our relationship or any goodwill to make the sale. So, I had to do what all good salespeople do—put myself in her shoes and think through what made her tick, what she most cared about, and how I could make her life better (or at least easier). I realized our primary shared goal was to get me off welfare, which made my getting an education a perfect candidate for achieving the goal. But how to help her see that alignment and agree to support my vision? You can't rely on people to intuitively understand your ideas' potential and impact, because they won't. That's just not how things work. You have to think through how someone who doesn't share your deep understanding of and commitment to your vision will hear it, think about it, and respond to it. Then you have to think through how to *shape* how they hear, think about, and respond to it. You convince the doubters by knowing every detail of your vision (or whatever you are selling) and having supreme confidence in and commitment to it.

I sat down and thought through my caseworker's potential objections. "Welfare is designed to cover basic expenses, not luxuries like college." "What if you lose interest in college before getting your degree and the money is wasted?" "What if you run out of money?" I realized playing defense would only get me part of the way, though, so I flipped the script from being a defensive presentation to one with that positive outcome that she would care about—getting me off welfare. I painted a vision in which the end result was my becoming a productive member of society rather than a drag. Being able to present my vision as something that she wanted just as much as I did allowed me to have confidence when I was selling it to her.

When you are selling your vision, however, it's important to remember that it's often an iterative process rather than a single event in time. If you really believe in your vision, you must have the courage and stamina to overcome the obstacles and objections that will no doubt be in your way. When I brought my vision of attending college to my former professor, he scoffed and didn't even give it a moment's consideration. I could have thought to myself, *He's right—what was I even thinking?* and given up after that interaction. But I didn't. He had given me the information I needed to create the financial foundation I would need to start turning my vision into a real plan when he pointed me to social services. When I brought my vision to my caseworker, her first objection was one I hadn't even considered—how I would manage Eric while I was in class. Again, I could have given up. She was right and I hadn't thought through daycare for Eric, let alone its impact on my budget. Rather than giving up, however, I went back to the drawing board to find the solution.

Each of these objections could have been vision killers if I let them be. I could have said, "This is impossible," and given up, but I had faith that the vision was the right one for me and that it was achievable. So, I built off the obstacles I encountered to improve my plan, and eventually, through adaptation and perseverance, I succeeded.

When I secured my caseworker's approval to attend college, I was elated! I almost couldn't believe it! I felt liberated and, for the first time in a while, I felt hope. I had a vision that inspired and motivated me, and against all odds, I had convinced someone to support me in achieving it! Making that sale meant I was beginning to transform my potential into my reality.

Like anything, practice makes perfect. As I began to succeed in selling my visions—first to my caseworker, then to my professors, employers, and beyond—I gained confidence and got even better at selling. This lesson has played out hundreds of times in my career. In fact, I have never stopped selling visions, from my earliest days in that trailer all the way through serving as CEO and chairing boards of directors of multinational companies.

So, have the confidence to start selling your vision to your superiors, colleagues, and team members. If you truly believe in and desire your vision, and act out of that conviction, you will draw others to you and they will join you on the path to achieving it as the vision becomes everyone's goal line, not just yours.

Chapter 2

Taking Flight (1973–1975)

By the early spring of 1973, I could finally see the Orange County Community College finish line coming into view. I looked forward to graduating and starting to put all the knowledge and skills I had worked hard for over the past three years into practice. And I was looking forward to making some real money! So, with a few months of school left, I started looking for my first professional job.

I had excelled at OCCC, so I felt pretty confident going into the job search. I was a strong student and was on track to graduate with a 4.0 GPA in the engineering curriculum. I had held a number of leadership positions on campus—from president of the Engineering and Technology Society, to being a popular student senator, to being a photographer for the yearbook and school newspaper. And my professors were very encouraging about my job prospects.

As I began my search, I wasn't very picky. I just wanted a job where I could be an electronics technician and could drive to work in less than an hour. Terry and I had married a couple of months earlier, and Eric and I had moved out of our trailer and into Terry's house in Circleville, New York. He had an older two-story home, well-situated on 11 acres, with a pond and room for horses, which were a long-time passion of mine. He also had three boys from his first marriage, so I was suddenly the mother in a family of six.

Our local electric company, Orange & Rockland Utilities, had an office in Middletown, New York, near our home, and since they would almost certainly need technicians they were my first target. I drove to the office, filled out an application, and was disappointed when the receptionist told me they weren't really hiring anyone as I handed my application to her. I'm not sure if they even looked at my application before they called me back to reiterate that there were no openings. I was obviously disappointed, but also a little shocked. I figured that since I had done so well in college, people would jump to hire me (I guess I was a little naïve back then). After all my A's in class, I was not pleased to get an F on my first attempt on the job front. I began to wonder if finding a position wasn't going to be as easy as I thought. I was confident in my abilities, but those abilities wouldn't matter much if there were no jobs available.

I had heard that there was a big IBM plant in Fishkill, New York, about 45 minutes away across the Hudson River. I hadn't seen any job postings so I wasn't sure if they were hiring either, but IBM would be a dream job for any newly minted electronics technician, so it was at least worth a try. So, I drove to the facility to make a cold call on the receptionist to see if I could get lucky. As I entered the lobby, I was confronted by a sea of men in suits and badges bustling about with serious looks on their faces. It was an exciting and impressive scene to this young woman just starting out in her career. I walked up to the receptionist, explained why I was there, and then sat down to fill out an application, hoping IBM would be more impressed by my accomplishments than Orange & Rockland had been. When I turned the application in, the receptionist told me they would "be in touch," but her noncommittal tone didn't leave me feeling very confident or optimistic as I walked out of the building.

On the drive home, I started to prepare myself for the likely second rejection. IBM just seemed out of my league. The facility was so impressive, and I figured they probably didn't need someone fresh out of college for whatever important work was going on behind those guarded doors. Still, I was proud of myself and glad I had visited and dropped off my application. *Oh well. Onward and upward*, I thought to myself.

When I got home and opened my front door, however, the phone was ringing. I dropped my bag and keys and rushed to get to the phone before it stopped. I breathlessly answered, "Hello?" It was IBM. I couldn't believe that they were getting back to me so quickly! In the 45 minutes since I had left, they had reviewed my application and decided to have me come back the next week for an interview. Six interviews for six different departments, to be precise. In retrospect, I think they instinctively jumped at the opportunity to hire a woman with a 4.0 GPA.

At the time, though, I was shocked! Six interviews! Surely at least one of those interviews would lead to a job offer. I was still on cloud nine when I drove back the next week for my day of interviews. I clearly remember that day. Well, I remember the day's *excitement* clearly. As I walked from interview to interview and met team after team, the actual events of the day kind of ran together. It was all so new to me—the technologies, the responsibilities, and even the language they used. It was impressive sounding, but it was hard to know exactly what I would be doing and how the different positions were really different from each other. What I noticed, however, was that they seemed to be spending a lot more time trying to sell me on IBM and their departments than I was spending trying to sell them on me. They seemed genuinely excited to have me come work for IBM. That felt nice, and in the end, I was offered jobs with four of the six departments.

It was great to have my pick of the jobs, but it wasn't an easy decision. They all paid the same—$210.00 per week, which was less than the AT&T offer I had received in school, but still a staggering amount of money to me (and more than anyone else I knew was making). They all came with the same title—Senior Laboratory Technician (entry level was technically "Laboratory Technician," but my experience in OCCC's astronomy lab and helping Terry at the radio station had given me a leg up). They even all focused on the same area — developing the technologies that would allow IBM to create the world's very first automated semiconductor manufacturing line. Ultimately, I had to go with my gut feeling about the labs and teams I'd be working with rather than on any job's specific role or duties.

I remembered that one department, with the less-than-exciting name of Department 71H, stood out from the others. It was focused on the interfaces that would connect IBM's System 7 computers to the manufacturing machines and robots; essentially the nervous system connecting the brain to the arms and legs of the new manufacturing line. Its lab looked state-of-the-art and its technicians seemed to have more power and latitude than the technicians in the other departments. It was the only department that brought its senior technicians to the interview process (all the other departments' interview teams consisted solely of engineers), and it seemed like those technicians, Al and Tom, ran the show in their labs. As a technician, that appealed to me. I also liked that there were schematic diagrams *everywhere* — taped on every wall and even spilling onto the floors. Amid all the schematics, though, there was a topographical map of Fishkill on the wall, which I also liked since I had always loved maps. The chemistry of it all just felt right so I decided to accept the position in Department 71H and celebrated my decision by going out and buying my first ever new car; a beautiful red Toyota Corona station wagon.

As it turned out, it was good that I proactively pursued a job after graduation, because the economy was still weak and the company recruiters who typically descend like locusts on colleges every spring never came because no one was hiring. Actually, after IBM offered me a job, the company did come to OCCC to see if they could hire other graduates as well. I think IBM's arrival surprised the OCCC guidance counselors because they were all scrambling at the last minute to set up appointments with their students. IBM ended up hiring five or six of my classmates, including my lab partner from that first engineering class, Jack (he was actually my lab partner in *every* class!).

I started at IBM the Monday after the weekend I graduated. Jack and my peers took a week off between graduation and starting to work, but I was in a hot hurry to get to work and start making some real money for the first time in my life! I arrived that morning in pigtails and a fashionably short skirt. While the men at IBM had a strict dress code (the white shirt and skinny black tie for which they were famous), there were no other women technicians or engineers to model a dress code for me to follow. So, I figured I would create the standard by dressing the way I wanted.

I was giddy as I was ushered to a room to have my picture taken for my new badge. When I got the badge, I noticed that mine was different from other people's badges. It had a green stripe across it, which I learned meant that I was working on a special IBM project (the FMS, or "Future Manufacturing System"). That was pretty cool, but it was even cooler when I discovered that the green stripe also allowed me to cut the line and have priority at "the crib," IBM's shop of parts and devices that engineers and technicians could raid as they were constructing their systems.

The rest of that first morning consisted of various orientation meetings about the company, benefits, and the like. I was excited about everything, and despite already being a mom and stepmom to four boys, the fact that I was now earning a salary and receiving benefits that could support my family filled me with pride and made me feel like a grown-up for the first time in my life.

After lunch, I was shown to my lab bench and met the senior technician who would supervise my work, Al from the interview process. When we met, he let me know I was coming into the

department in the middle of a whirlwind. Before I had arrived, IBM engineers had conducted a feasibility study and created a prototype of an automated semiconductor manufacturing line to demonstrate that automated manufacturing was possible. Well, the line wasn't working, and the possibility of automated manufacturing was now in question. The primary obstacle was the tremendous electronic noise, or interference, on the factory, or "fab," floor that disrupted the manufacturing tools' operation, causing them to malfunction and shut the line down. Al and the other senior technician from the interview, Tom, had been brought in to diagnose what was going wrong and to fix it. I arrived just as they were coming to the conclusion that the entire control system was flawed and needed to be redesigned. That explained why I had seen schematics all over the floor during the interview process; they were in the midst of solving the problems and redesigning the line.

I had already decided that I would act like an engineer at IBM (rather than a technician) since that was my ultimate career goal. Today, they would call this approach "Fake it 'til you make it." Little did I know that whether I planned to act like an engineer or not, I was going to be placed in that role on my very first day. Al came over to my bench and asked me to design and document a printed circuit board (PCB) that would be able to automatically detect machine malfunctions on the manufacturing line. Basically, the PCB would need to be capable of receiving a bunch of inputs from the line and if something wasn't working right, it would need to display an error light. I was shocked to be given such a task on my first day! I thought it was a test to see how much I had learned at OCCC and whether I really knew my stuff. I only found out it wasn't a test after I turned my design in to Al for review and discovered it was assigned an IBM part number and put into production the very next day! That was incredible! I was doing engineering and generating real value on day one!

My next task was to design an analog-to-digital converter card that could take real-world phenomena like speed and pressure and convert them into digital bitstreams that the line computers could understand. Basically, I was helping the robots understand the world around them and respond appropriately. On an expensive automated semiconductor manufacturing line, the robots can't be running around like bulls in a china shop. It was a challenging assignment—one on the very edge of what I knew how to do—but I worked on the project, learning as I went. I spent the next six months researching, selecting, and securing the components that would go on the card, prototyping my solution, and taking measurements to ensure it delivered the superior levels of accuracy we needed. When I was done, I was thrilled to see another one of my creations receive a part number and go into production. I still have that card sitting on my bookshelf at home and it makes me smile every time I see it.

I was developing a skill for jumping into projects and figuring out how to do them as I went along. It was scary sometimes, but I spent the rest of that first year at IBM designing and prototyping the Distributed Interface cards that would connect the computers controlling the manufacturing line and the machines on the line.

Another equally important skill I developed that year was how to work well with *everyone*. That was a significant part of my early success and paved the way to many of my future accomplishments. I focused on making friends with everyone in the building.

While some of my fellow technicians and engineers felt secretaries were beneath them, I went out of my way to befriend them. In many organizations, the executive assistants (EAs) are where the real power lies! When you need access to the "big bosses" in any organization, having their EA as one of your friends can be an invaluable asset. And when you have to go on a business trip, you will find yourself with better flights, hotel rooms, and meals if the secretary setting them up likes you! To this day, I still make it a point to befriend every administrative assistant I encounter.

Whenever I went to the crib to get the parts I needed, I took the time to get to know the people who worked there. I got to know their names. I asked about their lives and days. I smiled and had a positive attitude. And as a result, I always got preferential treatment. I got the parts I needed faster than anyone else, which made my managers very happy.

I even performed tasks that others considered beneath them in this drive to be on good terms with everyone. In those days, we still designed our circuit schematics with pencil and paper. That meant numerous trips to the copy room to make copies for review by others. One time when I was in the copy room making copies of my latest design, a male engineer came into the room, saw me standing at the copier, and assumed I was a secretary. He dropped a pile of papers on the table next to me and asked me to make copies for him. I suppose I should have been offended but I wasn't. It just wasn't that big of a deal, and I try not to sweat the small stuff. I decided to just make the copies since it wouldn't kill my day and I just might make another friend. I smiled and asked where his office was, saying, "I'll drop them off." He found out later that I was actually a senior technician and I like to think I expanded his mind a little bit that day.

Being one of the very few women in a male-dominated role, company, and industry, is not for the faint of heart. I was never intimidated by the situation, though. I had developed the confidence in myself and my skills to know that I could hold my own with any of my peers. But I was aware that most of them thought I was taking a job away from some "more deserving" male breadwinner. Don't get me wrong; there was never any disrespect or friction in the lab. Everyone liked me, treated me well, and acknowledged my valuable contribution to the team.

It was one of those weird situations where they would gripe about "women in the workplace" at the lunch table, but then treat me like "one of the guys" and depend on me when we got back to the lab.

If my first year at IBM was largely hardware-based and designing and prototyping circuit boards, my second year was software-based. We had to design the software to make the hardware do what we wanted it to do. Again, these were the early days of robotics and automation, and it was quite a thrill to write a few lines of code and watch your software cause some machine to come to life and perform a task. And it was a lot of fun! On some of our less productive nights, we would write code to make the line's semiconductor wafer transports crash into each other, just because we had that power, and it was cool! Despite our shenanigans, however, we were good at what we did. We ultimately fixed the line's automation problems and enabled IBM to remain at the forefront of semiconductor manufacturing. In fact, we were so successful that our department grew into three separate departments that year.

It was during this second year that I got pregnant with my daughter, Megan, and I convinced Terry to leave the radio station and come work at IBM. As I sat writing code day after day throughout my pregnancy, my colleagues teased me that our daughter would be a "citizen of IBM."

It was also during this time that I decided to go back to college to get a full bachelor's degree in electrical engineering. I was lucky enough to already be doing some engineering work, but I knew I would never be recognized (or promoted) as an engineer at IBM without the Bachelor of Science (BS). I told my boss my plan to take a leave of absence and go back to school full-time. Since I planned to come back, I would continue to receive my benefits, and IBM guaranteed that a job would be waiting for me when I finished my degree. But my decision to go back to school would end up being used against me that last spring before I left.

March was annual performance review time at IBM and when I went to meet with my boss, he told me that I had earned a "1," the highest possible appraisal within the IBM system. Basically, it meant they thought I walked on water. It was an amazing review and a strong affirmation of the quality and value of my work. I was excited because performance appraisals were also the primary measuring stick by which annual pay raises were determined. I started imagining how big my increase might be. My excitement was quickly doused, however, when my boss went on to say that since I was leaving to go back to school and since there were a lot of hard-working family men in the department who apparently "needed the money more than me," I wouldn't be receiving a raise that year. Not a penny. I was shocked, but I maintained my composure. I knew I could go above him to complain about my treatment, but I had two months left before I would be leaving and as I quickly weighed the pros and cons of venting my frustration, I realized it was a battle not worth fighting. I didn't think the IBM system would respond well to my rocking the boat and I wanted to come back once I finished my degree. I might win the pay raise battle, but I would lose the war. And I was in it to win the war. I thanked him for my review, got up out of my chair, and walked out.

Lesson #3 — Don't Sweat the Small Stuff

In the late 1990s, Richard Carlson published an immensely popular book, *Don't Sweat the Small Stuff...and It's All Small Stuff*, which launched a highly successful series of books as its philosophy resonated within our stressed-out world. Over the course of 100 brief chapters, Richard unpacked what it meant to "not sweat the small stuff." A few of his chapters, like "Ask Yourself the Question, 'Will This Matter a Year from Now?'"

and "Choose Your Battles Wisely," spoke to me because they expressed my lived experience.

As I stood there making copies of my latest circuit design, feeling pretty good about myself and looking forward to its review by my colleagues, I was shocked out of my reverie by the male engineer who assumed that I was a secretary because I was a woman. As the copier whirred away, I had a moment to decide whether I would be offended by his assumption and request that I make copies of his designs or whether this was small stuff. I had a moment to consider this one instance against the backdrop of my larger goals and aspirations. Would correcting the engineer and seeking an apology further my goal of advancing my engineering capabilities and reputation at IBM? What benefit would I gain by confronting his sexist assumption? The reality was that the only benefit would be to my ego, and it would definitely only be a small momentary victory in the larger war I would fight over the course of my career. Was my ego really so fragile that I needed to fight every battle, or was I strong enough to "choose my battles wisely"? Would I allow my ego to control my actions, and by extension my life, or would I choose to use my ego more productively?

We are living through an era where we have made much progress in women's rights and the rights of people of color and other marginalized individuals. At the same time, we are more easily offended than at any other time I can remember. Perhaps that's a sign of how much progress we have made; we can afford to be incensed by others' slights. But I can't help but think that there is still a long way for us to go and that we need to keep our eyes on the prize. Until women, people of color, and other marginalized individuals have full equity and access to opportunity, I don't have time to sweat the small stuff. I'm too busy working on the big stuff. In that war, indignance is a poison that weakens the offended person more than the person causing the offense, while humility and taking the high road is a battlefield advantage worth its weight in gold.

Some might view my decision to smile and agree to make the copies and drop them off at his office as "being a doormat," but there is a difference between acquiescing out of weakness or lack of courage and being confident enough in yourself and your value to keep your ego in check and to pick your battles.

Again, when I had my stellar last review at IBM before going back to school, but wasn't given any subsequent pay increase, I weighed the benefits of complaining about a month or two of lower wages versus being able to leave IBM with them thinking I walked on water. Yes, I was upset at the injustice, but I recognized once again that the only real damage was to my ego and that my ego was stronger than that. Over the course of my career, I have developed a thick skin against people's ill treatment of me, so long as it didn't interfere with my longer-term plan. I've never found that reacting impulsively to other people's errors in thinking has ever changed their minds or helped me achieve my larger goals. What changes people's minds is accomplishment and achievement. And that's what I focus on.

I found taking the high road came naturally to me. I know that isn't always the case for people, but it *is* a skill you can nurture and develop over time. It might take practice and you will make mistakes along the way, but as long as you keep your eye on your vision and the path to achieving it, you will make progress. And in time, all the small stuff will be revealed as such and shown to be beneath your response. The high road is the only road to true success in your career and life.

Chapter 3

Back to the Nest (1975–1976)

I finished those last two months at IBM, working right up to the Friday before I gave birth to my daughter on Monday, May 12, 1975, which coincidentally was *my* birthday as well. What a great birthday present—a baby girl to start to even the odds in my family of all boys!

I was now busy raising *five* children, but not too busy to slow down my dreaming and planning for my future career. I still wanted that BS in engineering, and I figured there was no better time to pursue it than now, while I was taking care of my daughter and not working.

Of course, not going back to work and enrolling in classes meant that we were going to have to be creative to make ends meet. We had been a two-income family, so losing one of those incomes was going to require some belt-tightening. In addition to frugality at home, I needed to figure out how to accelerate my course of study so I could return to the workforce as quickly as possible.

First, though, I needed to figure out where to go to school. My options were fairly limited since we lived in Middletown, New York, and I couldn't uproot the family to move somewhere else (and the days of remote learning were still decades in the future). Fairleigh Dickinson University was only an hour away and they offered the BS in electrical engineering technology that I wanted. I reached out to them and discovered to my pleasant surprise that they would accept all my engineering credits from OCCC and that my associate's degree in social sciences satisfied all of their liberal arts requirements as well!

With that bump, I figured I could squeeze the full bachelor's degree into just over a year by taking advanced calculus that first summer and 18 and 21 credits in the fall and spring respectively. I was going to have to get creative to get the *right* credits, though. Fairleigh Dickinson wouldn't offer enough engineering-specific courses in that one year for me to complete my curriculum requirements. With my usual fearlessness (or naïveté), though, I figured I would just get started and work out a solution along the way.

I enrolled at Fairleigh Dickinson University and got right to work on that calculus course two weeks after Megan was born. Now, calculus is never easy, but the compressed timeframe and pace at which it is taught during the summer is downright deadly. I was taking classes four nights a week and Megan got used to me cradling her with my left hand while my right hand deciphered calculus problems for hours on end that summer.

Once the fall semester started, I supplemented my undergraduate classes with a graduate-level night course in computer science to help me get enough engineering courses. That night class ended up being my favorite class that semester. The professor was a young, smart guy who had earned his undergraduate degree at the University of Moscow. He loved the fact that I had worked at IBM, and we spent hours outside class talking about computer architectures and how IBM could be even more successful in the emerging future of the minicomputer.

I also took a materials science course that fall. It was tough and I was really struggling. Well, the whole class was struggling. The professor was talking over everyone's heads. No one understood what he was teaching, and we were all getting poor grades. My classmates and I were griping about the situation during a class break, and by the end of the conversation I was elected to talk to the professor and see if I could convince him to slow down the pace of the class. I made an appointment to speak with the professor and as it turned out, he was as concerned as all of us. He didn't understand why we were struggling so much and was unsure about how he could help. I explained that the professor's accent and pace of teaching were making it difficult for us to absorb the material as rapidly as he was delivering it. He asked for my help, and as I helped him adjust his teaching style, I found myself on the receiving end of both the class's and the professor's gratitude.

As the fall semester progressed, I felt the looming pressure of needing 21 more engineering credits to graduate in the spring. Then one day, Terry came up from the basement after a day of tinkering and let me know that a new microprocessor was being released that only cost $25, which was a small fraction of the cost of the other microprocessors on the market. The MOS Technology 6502 wasn't fancy, but it was speedy, and Terry mused that it would be interesting to see if someone could use it to build a computer from scratch without breaking the bank. A lightbulb went off in my head—I could design my own course at Fairleigh Dickinson focused on building a computer! I would be able to enroll in 12 credits of engineering courses in the spring. The question was, could I convince my professors that building a computer warranted the additional nine engineering credits I needed to graduate that spring?

It was just another sales job for me, but I was up for the challenge. My professors all thought the idea of someone building a computer from scratch was basically "rocket science" — exciting, but extremely difficult. I could tell they had some doubts about whether I could pull it off, but I convinced the chair of the Electronics department to award me six credits for building the computer. That was great, but I was still three credits short. So, my next stop was my computer science professor, with the proposal that I write an interpreter, or the software that would make the computer accessible for higher-level programming. At this time, computers did not come with any software other than the binary code, the ones and zeros that made them tick. He agreed that if I could do it, it would be worth three credits. Success!

By the time the spring semester started in January 1976 I had a lot on my plate. I was caring for a family of seven, driving an hour each way to get to school to take 12 credits of classes, and building a computer in my spare time! Building the computer was sort of a family project, though. I was in charge of the microprocessor, its 64K of memory, and the interfaces to a Model 33 teletype keyboard (like the one I had seen Dr. Gard operating at OCCC) and printer, as well as a full panel of hexadecimal switches and lights that showed the computer's status and let me key in its instructions and data as 1s and 0s or hexadecimal code. Those 64K bytes of memory may seem insignificant considering the memory-hungry applications we all work with today, but at that time 64K seemed massive and no one could imagine what could be done with all that memory. I was thankful for and drew upon my experience at IBM as I started designing my computer. And while I was building my computer's brain and nervous system, Terry and our oldest son Barry took care of the computer's power supply and the streamlined case that would house the computer. While

Chris, Terry, and Barry go over the details of a program on the deck of their Jericho chalet. Barry did all the woodwork and finishing on the computer cabinet and some of the wiring and mechanical work on EC 1000.

we were building the physical computer, I was writing the machine code the microprocessor would use to operate. That was an unparalleled mental challenge, but it was a thrill as the computer came together and those lights and switches came alive! My daughter Megan, who was now almost a year old, was simply fascinated and delighted by the computer's pretty lights and sounds.

A month into the semester, I got an infection in my nose, which spread everywhere in my body, including my lungs. I developed a terrible case of staph pneumonia and ended up in the hospital. I was so sick that I was delirious most of the time, and my family was genuinely worried that I might not come home. After about five days of being totally out of it, though, I regained my senses. All I could think of was how much I missed my kids, especially Megan, who was only nine months old. After ten days in the hospital and about two pounds of antibiotics I finally got to come home. It was such a relief to be back with my family, but now I had to face the reality of those 21 credits that were still looming over me. I had to catch up on all I had missed at school, and I still had to get my computer fully operational! At that point, just walking 100 feet was exhausting, but I was determined to get it all done. Terry set up a big worktable with a light in our bedroom, and I locked myself away for hours every night to do my homework, and I worked on my computer every weekend.

When the semester finally ended in May, though, I aced all my final exams, and for my grand finale, I brought my computer to school to demonstrate to my professors and classmates. I called it the "EC1000," with the "EC" standing for "Engineering Change," figuring there would be *a lot* of engineering changes necessary before we got it right. Everyone was blown away by what I had been able to figure out and create on my own.

The EC1000 worked perfectly, and my interpreter positively hummed, opening up the computer's full programming potential.

Later in life, I would meet Apple's Steve Wozniak and learn that we had both been building computers at that time using that 6502 microprocessor. Of course, he was using it to build the first Apple computer! We talked about the binary codes we used to make the computer work, laughing that we were probably the only two people in the world who got a kick out of remembering old hexadecimal codes like 4C for "branch unconditional" to pass control to a different part of the program. We reminisced about how the 6502 could only handle 64K of memory and what a "dog" it was to design for as we wrote code to squeeze as much out of that memory as possible.

That experience of building a personal computer would give me a huge leg up when I returned to IBM. The new PCs were a microcosm of the big mainframe IBM computers, and designing one from scratch had given me insights into and experience with all aspects of a complete computing system. It turned out that I was one of the rare few at IBM, the biggest computer company in the world, who had that complete, big-picture computing perspective. Earlier computers had been built with teams of engineers, but now, affordable microprocessors made it possible for one person to design and understand a whole system, and I was one of the very small number of people at IBM who had actually done it.

But before I could return to IBM, I had to graduate from Fairleigh Dickinson, which I did in that one-year period, and with a 4.0 GPA. I left the school with a sour taste in my mouth, though. Since so many of my credits had come from OCCC, Fairleigh Dickinson would not allow me to graduate with the honors I had earned and join the other honors students at the front of the class at graduation. I pled my case to the university's administration and tried to get them to relent and let me walk with the rest of the honors students. I explained that I had taken a heavy course load, had earned a 4.0, and was only one Fairleigh Dickinson credit short of the minimum number they required, but they were steadfast and unwavering in their commitment to their rules.

Not being allowed to walk with the honor students was a bitter pill to swallow after all my hard work. Later in life, after I had risen to become the first female CEO of a semiconductor company and was a multimillionaire, Fairleigh Dickinson came calling during a fundraising campaign. They sent an alum to visit with me and draft an article about my career for the school magazine. During that interview, he asked me to contribute money to the school. I smiled and told him the story of my accelerated course of study and closed with my graduation experience. He was surprised by how I was treated, and probably *not* surprised when I later chose to contribute money to OCCC instead of Fairleigh Dickinson.

In the end, though, I had grasped my prize. I had graduated with a BS and 4.0 GPA in electrical engineering technology and was ready to return to IBM, which welcomed me with open arms and offered me a wide range of opportunities in which I could put my new credentials and skills to work.

Lesson #4 — Do the Work; There Are No Shortcuts

There's a funny saying, "Opportunity is missed by most people because it is dressed in overalls and looks like work." The humor of that adage is based in the assumption that, in general, people have an aversion to work. To be successful, however, there is no substitute for rolling up your sleeves and doing the work. To be clear, I'm not simply referring to the success that is measured by promotions and pay increases. I'm talking about a deeper and more abiding level of success that is gained through the skills and instincts you gain and develop as a result of doing work. The external rewards are nice, but ultimately, they are less valuable than the internal rewards of increased competence and capability.

When I set out to build my own computer at Fairleigh Dickinson during the earliest days of personal computing, I was signing up for work, *a lot of it*. I was going to have to determine all the component parts I would need (and which ones), how to connect and configure them, and how to develop the software layers to make them communicate and work successfully together. It took a tremendous amount of research and even more trial and error. I spent untold hours wrestling with my creation to get it to do what I needed it to do. In the end, however, I prevailed and delivered my prized EC1000.

Building my own computer allowed me to accumulate credits faster and accelerate along the path to my engineering degree, the external reward, but that wasn't the true value of having done all of that work. I didn't realize it at the time, but the true value lay in the internal reward of the deep understanding I gained in how a personal computer actually works, an understanding that very few people possessed at the time, even in the leading technology companies of the day. It was an understanding that was only possible through hours and hours of wrestling with the technologies, learning how they worked and didn't work at the base level and as an integrated system. *There are no shortcuts to that level of understanding.* It is only earned through hours and hours of effort and experience. Doing all that work—as difficult and, yes, frustrating as it was at times—gave me a skill set that shaped me and would have impact for years to come, long after my Fairleigh Dickinson diploma was packed away in a box somewhere in the basement. That awareness began to dawn on me when I got back to IBM and discovered I understood personal computing systems better than anyone else at one of the leading computing companies in the world.

At IBM and in most companies, you will find people who skate by on their credentials, relationships, or looks, but their success tends to be fleeting. Eventually, the ones who work hard will pull ahead of the rest of the pack.

Eventually, I moved into management and leadership at IBM, but I would never have been as successful as I was without spending years working in the bowels of the business, understanding how the engineering and technology worked at a deep level. Doing the work makes you so much more conversant as a leader because you begin to instinctively recognize and understand the patterns and connective tissue between discrete technologies and events. Years later as a manager and CEO, the understanding and instincts I had gained from my years as an engineer meant that I could quickly spot and intuitively grasp the risks and opportunities in our products and operations. That's something that a newly minted MBA (Master of Business Administration) graduate without my experience couldn't do. It allowed me to move faster and guide my teams more successfully. My earlier years of trial and error meant that there was less trial and error when I was a manager.[1]

I coach many executives (and aspiring executives), most of whom are already well into their careers in global organizations, but one conversation I had with someone at the beginning of their career happened while I was working on this book. I ride horses and compete in international cow cutting competitions (more to come on that in future chapters), and I was at a ranch for practice one morning. As I was waiting for my practice to begin, I was chatting with two young cowgirls. One of them was studying technology at a local school but was thinking about transferring to management studies. I shared my story with her and how understanding the technology made me a far better and more successful manager. I encouraged her not to skip the work on the way to the manager level. It doesn't have to be work in technology, but whatever field you choose, do the work. You can't shortcut the work if you want to achieve your full potential.

People naturally want success to come quickly. They are impatient and resistant to doing work. I get that, but my experience has demonstrated that work is the only path to reaching your full potential. That was the case in my career. It was the case in my personal life—whether with my family, as a dairy farmer, or as a cow cutting champion. Don't be afraid to start at the bottom and work your way up. The pace of your rise is less important than the strength of your rise, and strength is only built upon a foundation of effort and time.

Note

1   Well, there was still trial and error, but this time it was in how to be a better manager of people and teams. Having done the work, built capabilities, and achieved success before, however, I had the confidence and faith that I could do it again in new areas. And again, I discovered that being a great manager is almost impossible without years of doing the work of *actually* managing people.

Chapter 4

Back to IBM (1976–1980)

Since I planned to return to IBM after graduation, I maintained contact with my HR (human resources) rep during my year at Fairleigh Dickinson. Those conversations shifted from casual check-ins to more formal discussions about what my return to IBM would look like in the months leading up to graduation. They were holding a position for me at IBM, but the specific job and location were up for discussion. I could return to Fishkill, but I also had options in other facilities if I wanted. For the first time, I began to consider what opportunities might lie beyond the Hudson River Valley.

Bob Fiorenza had been my manager when I first joined IBM's 71H team in Fishkill, and he was promoted to be a second-line manager, or manager of managers, and transferred to IBM's facility in Essex Junction, Vermont while I was at Fairleigh Dickinson. IBM designed and manufactured a variety of memory chips in Vermont. Bob reached out to me before graduation to ask if I would consider moving to Vermont and joining one of his groups. I had never really thought about moving to Vermont, but I liked working for Bob, so I said I would consider it.

Terry and I drove up to Essex Junction in the spring to see the facility and discuss job opportunities with Bob. Vermont in the spring is gorgeous, and Essex Junction is a small town nestled in the rolling hills east of Burlington and Lake Champlain. As we drove up from New York, I was struck by the beauty of the state and, in retrospect, Bob didn't have to sell us awfully hard to get us to interview for positions there. And he sweetened the pot by letting us know that IBM would handle the sale of our house in New York, help us find and buy a new house in Vermont, and pay our moving expenses.

Bob's group was designing memory system cards while other groups in Essex Junction were designing the memory chips that went on the cards. One of his groups, however, was responsible for designing the systems to test the quality and performance of IBM's memory chips and cards. I thought that sounded interesting because building complete testers was more complex than designing cards and chips. In fact, those testers had to be orders of magnitudes more complex than the devices they were testing. It also required designing hardware *and* writing software code to make the whole system work. I had no idea how to actually build a tester, but as usual, that didn't stop me from giving it a try. So, when Terry and I were offered jobs in Vermont, we decided to make the move after I graduated.

When it was time, Terry, the kids, and I were all pretty excited. We were an outdoorsy family and Vermont, with its mountains, fields, and ski paths, seemed like heaven on earth. While we were waiting to move into our new house, we stayed at a local Holiday Inn in a room with two beds. It was the first time we had ever stayed in a hotel with the kids, and they did what all kids do the first time they stay in a hotel—jump onto the beds and bounce around with huge grins plastered across their faces. Terry looked on with dismay as I promptly joined them and his entire family bounced around like fools!

Rejoining IBM felt both new *and* familiar. I was starting a new job in a new facility, but being surrounded by male engineers in their IBM suits and badges again felt like a homecoming of sorts. When I arrived at my new lab and began meeting my colleagues and discussing the lab's latest work, I discovered that they were designing a new tester for the next generation of IBM memory cards and seemed to be almost as lost as I was. The existing testers weren't fast enough or able to handle the complexity of the new chips. Not to get too technical, but to fully test the chips, the testers would need to generate higher-resolution data patterns and highly precise, nanosecond timing to ensure the chips could handle the workload when they got out in the real world. As it turned out, my experiences automating IBM's semiconductor manufacturing line and in my recent classes gave me a leg up on my colleagues. I was equally surprised that I knew more than my senior peers and that they were willing to have a junior person take charge.

The immediate challenge we faced was developing the new tester's pattern and timing generators. I led the development of the timing generator, ultimately earning a patent for my design, and helped one of my colleagues design the new pattern generator. As I was working on these issues, though, I realized we could dramatically improve the testing process by automating it. All testers up to this point had been manual, meaning they had numerous physical switches that had to be manually programmed by engineers to execute the memory tests. It was a time-consuming process because doing it manually meant that every pattern had to be put in individually. My epiphany was that if we added a microprocessor to the testers and stored the test process in some form of memory, we could fully automate the testing process. No one had ever considered automating testing before, but doing so could reduce the time it took to test memory chips by a factor of hundreds, and maybe even thousands!

I set out to design IBM's first automated tester using the same 6502 microprocessor I had used in my EC1000 computer. I also ran to my local Radio Shack to purchase a cassette player and stack of cassette tapes to serve as the storage for the test process steps. In a couple of months, I had a prototype automatic tester and was running tests on IBM's cutting-edge 256K memory cards with my trusty 6502 microprocessor and a Radio Shack cassette recorder!

The next step was convincing the design engineers to use the automated tester and training them on how to use it and program their tests into the system. I thought it might be a challenge, but they were falling over themselves to use it when they realized the automated process would save them so much time. It was funny to watch these nerdy engineers running around with cassettes in their shirt pockets (along with their pocket protectors), knowing that the cassettes contained test patterns rather than Led Zeppelin or The Rolling Stones! I was surprised at how quickly the engineers learned how to operate the system, and even more so when they learned to use it better than I could! In the end, the new automated tester was a huge success, accelerating my career at IBM as a bit of a maverick who could approach problems in an unconventional way and typically find a better solution.

I was also increasingly gaining the confidence to question the status quo. At the time, IBM had a rigid preference for its own homegrown solutions and a prejudice against anything that was "not from here." While that allowed IBM to develop excellent integrated solutions, it meant that everything took longer and was more expensive. I knew we could dramatically speed up the process and significantly cut costs by using external, industry-standard components in our products. So, I sat down and wrote a paper, "How to Build an IBM Computer Without Even Trying," to describe my idea of using non-IBM parts and the time and cost savings it could generate for IBM. I started presenting my paper at internal IBM conferences and the response was very positive. I quickly realized, however, that the audiences were more interested in me as a young female engineer than in the contents of my paper. After my presentations, I would routinely have male engineers come up to tell me my paper was interesting, but what they really wanted was to ask me out to dinner!

The next time I spoke out against the status quo had a bigger impact. Bob was away on a business trip one week, so the facility's lab director, Art Strube, asked me to represent Bob's groups in a meeting about IBM's microprocessor strategy with the site's top management. I still remember the excitement I felt following Art into the cushy boardroom with its mahogany table, leather chairs, and artwork on the walls. I think they were all surprised to see me (since I wasn't Bob) and I dutifully took a spot along the wall as the meeting began.

After the discussion had been underway for a while, I began to realize that the executives didn't really understand how microprocessors worked within a larger system. They were thinking about microprocessors in isolation and recommending designs that operated at the wrong voltages to ever be useful in an actual application. It appeared that they had been developing IBM homegrown microprocessors for the sake of developing the latest hot technology rather than with any end application in mind, let alone a plan to make money and get a return for their R&D (research and development) investments.

I knew they were headed down a wrong, potentially costly path, but I didn't know what to do. I wanted to say something, but I was many levels below these company leaders. These executives were my boss's boss's bosses! But I couldn't stay quiet. I could feel the sweat trickling down my back as I raised my hand and they all looked at me in surprise. When I was called on, though, I plowed ahead, explaining the weaknesses of the current strategy as I saw them. I recommended a more application-focused strategy that emphasized uniform interfaces that would allow our microprocessors to connect to other components and larger systems more easily.

While the room was surprised that this upstart engineer that they had never even heard of would dare to speak up in the meeting, they recognized the logic of my perspective, and my success using microprocessors to automate chip testers gave me credibility. They sat up and listened to me intently. That experience, more than anything else, thrust me into the spotlight and crowned me the facility's microprocessor expert.

I was labeled a "high potential" engineer and asked to train the site's other engineers on the relatively new technology.

Word came down from the executive ranks that they wanted me to design a course on microprocessors for IBM's continuing education program. Despite the added workload, I enjoyed it and my class was an instant hit and regularly oversubscribed. After training the first few groups of engineers, though, I grew tired of the teaching role (or at least the subject) and handed it off to others to continue.

Over the next couple of years, we built four or five generations of the automated testers I designed. Beyond that, other manufacturing groups working on their own memory chips' testers were also using my designs and components, so my influence at Essex Junction grew rapidly and far beyond my department.

It was about this time that Terry and I started having marital problems. He had been hired in another group working on different test equipment. IBM would hire couples, but they separated us and had us work in different groups. While that was undoubtedly wise, it allowed an unintended competition to emerge between Terry and me. I was the only woman engineer and as I got better and better at what I was doing and gained more and more courage to go against the tide, I was getting a lot of visibility in the organization and was seen as a "rising star." I think my rapid rise bruised his ego on the way up.

Being a woman, IBM focused intensely on my career development. I was one of the very few examples IBM had that demonstrated "equal opportunities" for men and women, and since I was good at what I did, I was placed on a "fast track" development plan and guided toward a program that would teach me more about the business. To be honest, I wasn't all that interested. At that time, I just wanted to be an engineer, not a manager. But they were persistent, so I eventually left the world of testers to enter program management as a program development manager.

Well, that was boring. I never felt much of a sense of accomplishment or achievement. Certainly not like when I was an engineer. But I plodded through that to the next step on my career development path, a stop at the strategy department to discuss and design IBM's microprocessor strategy. Again, I found that exceedingly boring. We weren't really doing anything; we were just *talking* about doing things. I was an engineer! I wanted to create things!

I increasingly found myself traveling a path that didn't interest me. I was following the guidance of IBM management to expand my capabilities, but the capabilities I was adding were boring. I began to wonder why I was doing something I didn't care about. Plus, the growing competition between me and Terry was just making life miserable. I decided I needed to take a break and try something new.

That "something new" meant leaving IBM—my home for my entire professional career up until that point—and starting my own company. It was a highly unusual decision at the time. These were the days before leaving a well-paying, established job to launch a startup was really a thing. But I figured, *Why not?* Terry had a good job with benefits. Megan was five, and starting a company would allow me to be home with her more, so Terry and I discussed the opportunity and decided I should give it a shot. And so I left IBM.

Lesson #5—Where There Is an Opening, Go for It!

I have never been very inspired by the "popular" in business or life. I tend to become bored quickly by the market, business, and investment opportunities that everyone else is focused on. My thinking is that if everyone else is already doing it, whatever value may have been there at one time is quickly eroding as increasing numbers of people slice and dice up the opportunity and fight over the scraps. I'm more excited about and motivated by finding the undiscovered gem or opportunity that others haven't spotted or acted upon yet. The moments of greatest acceleration in my career and life have come in the pursuit and capture of the "white spaces" of undiscovered and uncertain opportunity.

When I realized there was an opportunity to dramatically improve the efficiency of the chip-testing process through automation, *and that no one else had ever thought of doing that before*, I jumped in with both feet! I didn't hesitate for a moment to begin designing and creating a prototype, even running to my local Radio Shack to buy the cassette recorder and tapes I would need! Once I had my prototype, I poured myself into convincing the engineers of the value of my new process, and it took off like wildfire. White spaces, successfully acted upon, are always exciting. When I saw and acted upon that opening, my reputation grew rapidly at IBM. I was seen as someone who "thought outside the box" and was willing to strike out on my own in pursuit of an idea that I thought had potential. It differentiated me from all the other engineers who had stayed in the "colored-in spaces" that were well-known and understood—and unimaginative and limited.

When I sat nervously in that microprocessor strategy meeting, listening to managers who were several layers above me in the organization laying out a strategy that I knew wouldn't work, or wouldn't work as well as they hoped, I could have kept quiet and gone with the flow. Certainly, that was what was expected of me. But I couldn't ignore that opportunity to once again step into the white space and explore a better path forward. And once again, it dramatically accelerated my career. I became the site's "microprocessor expert," and was asked to develop and teach a microprocessor class to the other engineers. Of course, once it became popular, my interest waned, and I was ready to move on to the next white space.

The white spaces are always where the greatest opportunity lies, if you have the courage to seek them out and pursue them. I say courage because if it didn't take courage, more people would do it. People don't naturally look for the white spaces because we are creatures of habit and everything and everyone around us encourages us to stick with what works, to follow the accepted and prescribed paths to success. Organizations, like organisms, evolve over time to follow "what works," accreting a solid foundation of "the tried and true." While that foundation provides security, it also constrains the organization's and its people's vision of the future. The wise person, though, recognizes that the future will undoubtedly be different from the past. They are aware of the accepted paths but not limited to them. Like a pioneer, you must blaze your own way. Sometimes, it will keep you in those well-worn paths, but sometimes, you will spot something off the trail, maybe on the horizon, and you need to be brave enough to explore it if you feel there is value in it.

As you begin seeking out the white spaces and acting on the opportunities, you will find that success is self-reinforcing. That first step into a white space in your career will be scary. It is completely unknown, and all the external forces are arrayed against you. But once you achieve success with that first white space, you gain the internal fortitude to know you can do it again. Each subsequent success compounds your courage and, if you successfully execute on those opportunities, your value to your organization and those around you will accelerate and be unbounded.

You might think that white spaces are limited, that they are a diminishing resource and that with every successfully executed opportunity, the remaining pool of opportunity is less. In my experience, however, there is always more white space to be discovered (but that doesn't make every white space valuable). The backdrop against which we are operating is not static; it is dynamic and constantly evolving. White space and opportunity can be abundant in times and places of chaos—a frequent occurrence in today's world. White spaces that were not there yesterday can appear today, and the white spaces that are here today may not be there tomorrow.

For white-space hunters like me, there is always opportunity, and the only limits are our own imagination, creativity, and ambition. While I have been speaking about white spaces within my technical world, the principle holds in every discipline and area of life. The English teacher who notices a gap in his school's curriculum where dyslexic students are not being well served, and studies to become an Orton-Gillingham or Wilson specialist, is stepping into the white space. The brewery that adds a coffee shop in the morning hours to more productively use their space is stepping into the white space. Again, not every opportunity is worthwhile, but when you see something and have the conviction that it is worthwhile, have the courage to go for it. As Nike said, "Just do it!"

Chapter 5

Taking Flight on My Own (1980–1984)

I left IBM in 1980 to start my own company.

There were a number of solid reasons why I left IBM—I was bored with the opportunities in IBM's "fast track" development plan, workplace competition with Terry was exacting a toll on our marriage (and me personally), and Megan was almost five years old. I really wanted to spend more time with her in those formative years. But the decision to go from IBM to starting my own company was quintessential Chris King—I figured I had enough skills to get started and that I would figure it out as we went along!

It started as a "family and friends" project, with Terry and the boys (especially the oldest, Barry) pitching in, and even my best friend Jack stopping in on nights and weekends to give us a hand. We knew there was a lot of white-space potential to use microprocessors to control and automate machines outside semiconductor manufacturing and we thought that my trusty EC1000 would give us a great start. I mean, how many other people had a fully functional personal computer in 1980?

So, we huddled around the dining room table one evening to dream up our company. First things first—what to name it? It all felt like an exciting adventure, and being an outdoorsy family, we quickly decided that "Expedition" should be at least part of the name.

Next, what would our company actually do? At that time, we were still in the earliest days of what was possible with computer technology; opportunity lay all around us, but since it was all new, we didn't know where to start. We looked around at real-world processes that could be improved through automation and settled on building a computer-controlled system for the design and manufacture of signs for businesses and the like. Basically, we were leveraging microprocessors and my experience to create one of the first Computer-Aided Design (or CAD) systems where you could create the sign concept on the computer and then interface it to sign-making equipment.

So, I wrote up a business plan, took it to the local Small Business Association, and convinced them to give us a $20,000 loan. Knowing we would likely need more money to reach break-even, and feeling confident in our prospects, we took out a second mortgage on our home for an additional $25,000, which seemed like a lot of money at the time.

And with that, we launched Expedition Graphics. My first job as president was to build my team. I could handle the hardware development as we were getting started, but I needed someone to develop the software to really make things sing. I also needed a secretary/accountant and a lawyer to keep us out of trouble! Fortunately, people flocked to work with us, not because we could pay them well (we couldn't!), but because we were doing something new and interesting, and they wanted to be part of it.

My second job was to find some office space for us to work; we didn't have room to keep working in my basement. We found and rented a great space over a liquor store (complete with a hairdresser next door) in Jericho, Vermont, where we were living at the time. Our small team of five moved in and got right to work.

It didn't take long, though, before we realized that designing and producing our system was going to take quite a while. My heart sank as I ran and reran the projections and realized that what I thought was a "huge" startup financing cushion would be gone before we would have a product in manufacturing. We had a good idea and knew how to execute it, but it would just take too long to get to market. The painful truth stared me in the face as I went over those spreadsheets—we would need to pivot or expand the scope of our business if we were going to avoid running out of money.

Then fate smiled upon us. A German company, Karl Süss, called our office one afternoon and I answered the phone. They had come to Vermont to start a business designing semiconductor manufacturing tools, had already acquired a large manufacturing site in Waterbury, Vermont, and had designed the tools' physical mechanics, but they needed help designing the electronics and writing the software to control the tools. They wanted to work with a local company and had called our Small Business Association, who gave them our name (that small business loan ended up being valuable on multiple levels!). They asked if I would come and talk to them.

I jumped in the car and drove to Waterbury to meet with their top technical guy. It would be another "sell" job for me— they weren't looking to manufacture signs—but as I listened to what they needed, I was transported back to my semiconductor manufacturing line automation days and knew that solving their problems wouldn't be a problem for us. Basically, we would be creating another microprocessor-based system to control a machine. I demonstrated that we were a good fit for their needs, they hired us, and we got started on what promised to be an interesting project.

We quickly discovered a big hurdle, though. They were using Siemens hardware and all the manuals were in German! None of us spoke German, so we ended up hiring a full-time translator to help us with our work and with communications with our technical peers at Karl Süss. Beyond the translator, we would also need a bigger team to do all the work. As I started looking for people, I tried to hire bright people who were up for a challenge but hopefully didn't have a family to support, because our business was such high risk. I looked for single people or individuals who had a spouse working at a "real" job.

Meanwhile, with "all hands on deck" working on the Karl Süss project, our initial goal of developing our graphics system for signs languished. But that business wasn't going to make it anyway and I thought that if Karl Süss was willing to pay us to develop a microprocessor-driven system, there must be other companies who needed us to do the same things. We could pivot and market our company as an "electronics design for hire" company. It was worth a shot, at least.

With our pivot, I realized we would need a new name for the company! And just like that, Expedition Graphics became Expedition Electronics. That sounded good—I liked the alliteration and the name flowed well. If we were going to make a go of this, though, we would need a brochure to tout our broader capabilities, and we would need a sales and marketing lead to get us out there. Debbie Burke, who had just received her MBA, agreed to become our new head of sales and marketing. So, while we focused on finishing up the Karl Süss project, Debbie worked on and published our sales brochure, and began cold-calling potential customers and hitting the road to meet them.

Finally, the Karl Süss electronics were complete and working in Vermont. It ended up being a tough job, but the Germans were masters in the mechanics, and we kept up our end of the bargain by designing world-class electronics and clean, functional software. The next step was to assemble the final system in Germany. I had never been out of the United States before, so the night flight to Germany was quite exciting and a little scary. In 1981, there were very few people who spoke English in the area outside Munich where Karl Süss was located. It was a real challenge to communicate with my engineering counterpart through a non-technical interpreter, but we both spoke the language of engineering and we bonded over my test equipment. I had a simple system-continuity checker, which was a "bug" light that would let me know if there was a connection or not. That fascinated him, so when we finished our work together, I gave it to him and made a fast friend.

As we finished up the Karl Süss project, Debbie's work on sales leads for our new Expedition Electronics began to bear fruit and customers started to come in fast and furious. Companies started calling us to develop microprocessor-based design services for everything from digital scales and measuring equipment to medical devices to printed circuit boards and semiconductor manufacturing tools.

Our most memorable project was the Ladd Intracranial Brain Pressure Monitor. You only needed this brain pressure monitor if you were in dire straits and doctors had to relieve pressure on your brain during or after brain surgery or as the result of a traumatic brain injury. It was a complex system, and even though I was the president of the company, I would roll up my sleeves and work into the wee hours of the morning to make the system work. It was all-consuming work, and when I did get to sleep at night, I would have dreams that I had been injured in a car accident and they were going to use the Ladd Monitor on me. I woke up yelling, "No! No! No!" because I knew how many flaws we were working on in that system and I certainly didn't want it used on me!

By this time, we had grown to a team of about 25, all with differing levels of experience and skills. To me, it felt like we were a real going concern, but I knew that we would still look like small potatoes to any of our clients when they came to visit. So, whenever a new customer came to audit our operations, I would have all my friends come in to work so we looked like a larger operation. It was like we were on a movie set—when the customer was gone, we all cheered and yelled, "Break the set!"

The new customers kept rolling in, and one of the most notable was my old company, IBM. Since I left the facility at Fishkill, New York, IBM had manufactured thousands of Distributed Interface cards, a number of which I had actually designed. Many of those generations of cards were now having technical problems and they needed someone knowledgeable to debug and fix them. Obviously, we were perfect for the job— and we charged them a lot for fixing each card! We especially relished sending the finished product back to IBM in reused liquor boxes from the store downstairs. We thought our peers at IBM would get a kick out of that!

New customers would frequently call the shop with technical questions or concerns, and the calls were usually routed to me. When I answered, and the customer heard a woman's voice, they would often assume I was a secretary and ask to be connected to someone who "knew something." I would simply respond by asking them what they wanted, and then blow them away with all the technical information they could handle. They always calmed down and were appreciative of my responses and insights.

On the business side of the business, I enjoyed keeping track of our sales achievements, proudly graphing our income every month, which was oftentimes $1 million or more. But running the business was harder than designing chips and boards. As the president, I would bid on new jobs. If I bid too high, we wouldn't get the business and I would have to lay off people. If I bid too low, we might not have the money to pay people for their hard work. That was always stressful for me.

One thing we quickly learned was the importance of getting our projects done on time. We were working with companies to design their flagship products on extremely tight deadlines to meet their marketing plans and the timing of whenever their next big industry conference was held. That put a lot of pressure on me and my small team. Plus, we didn't get paid until we finished the job, which was a significant motivator to move fast! Despite our speed, though, things always came down to the wire, and I would literally wait at the mailbox outside our building to watch for the mailman, hoping he would deliver the checks from our customers so we could pay our people and taxes. It made me a little nostalgic for IBM. There was never this kind of financial pressure at IBM; everything was relaxed.

Eventually, the stress of making our income meet our expenses began to wear on me, and our Board of Directors regularly pointed out that our margins were so thin, we would easily run into the red. After four years of struggling to make ends meet, the future didn't appear to be getting any more profitable. Our board suggested that perhaps we should execute a "controlled crash," in which we would continue to work with our customers but at the same time cut back on expenses and prepare to slide gracefully out of business. While it was a little disappointing to let go of something for which I had been working so hard, it frankly sounded like a good plan to me.

It had been a hard four years, but during that time, I learned things I never would have learned if I had stayed at IBM. I learned how to start a company from scratch and run a razor-thin margin business. I learned how to manage the responsibility of being the ultimate decision-maker and having the buck stop with me. And most critically, I learned the importance of completing projects on time if you want to get paid. There was no room for complacency. Throughout the rest of my career, that unyielding drive to move fast with purpose would serve me well. No one else at IBM had a clue about the pace and pressures of the real world.

As we wound the business down and I worked to pay off our small business loan and second mortgage, I spent time reflecting on the four years and wondering what I would do next. Over the past four years, I had the luxury of spending more time with Megan (although she spent a lot of her time outside of school at the "business"). That said, things with Terry hadn't gotten any better over the four years. We were no longer competing at IBM, but the Expedition Electronics journey didn't help us to grow any closer. Ultimately, my marriage to Terry ended. We got a divorce and I moved into a rental house with Eric and Megan. Fortunately, my continuing friendship with Jack was a bright spot during this difficult period.

Around this time, my head of marketing, Debbie, heard about a microprocessor seminar being hosted by a company called Martindale Associates outside of Boston. Martindale was a distributor of system components powered by microprocessors like the systems I had worked on during my first years at IBM. They focused primarily on systems made by ProLog out of Monterey, California.

I thought the seminar might be a good chance to meet potential customers who needed microprocessor expertise, so Debbie and I got in the car and headed to Boston. We arrived as a ProLog engineer was kicking off the seminar, and as was typical, we were the only women in a classroom full of male engineers. When it was time for Q&A, I had a question about how the ProLog system handled interrupts, or breaking into the normal flow of operations for some other necessary operation. When I raised my hand and asked my question, the technical depth of my inquiry stumped the ProLog engineer, and he didn't really have an answer. Suddenly, a curly-headed young man strode up the aisle from the back and gave me a thorough answer to my question.

I would later learn that the young man's name was Brad Paul, and he was a partner at Martindale Associates. He was only in his twenties, but it was clear he was the technical brain behind Martindale's Massachusetts operations. After the seminar, Brad and I struck up a conversation and bonded over a myriad of technical subjects. We agreed to meet again, and in our follow-up conversation, Brad and his partner asked if I would work with them to provide local technical support for the ProLog products. I would later discover that Brad was the star salesman for ProLog products and won their top salesperson of the year award every year. Since they would be another paying customer, I of course agreed, and Brad started calling me into his technically difficult customer calls. Brad and I were a great team, with him playing the role of sales guy, and me as the technical "heavy hitter."

As Expedition Electronics' days were coming to an end, Brad invited me to the annual ProLog sales meeting held in Monterey, California. At the meeting, I was exposed to the full depth and breadth of ProLog product applications—everything from rides at Disney to industrial weighing systems. One of the conference's fun activities was a contest to see who could present the best application for ProLog's cards. The Martindale team coaxed me to enter, and at dinner on the last night of the conference, I presented my design for a ProLog system to run a computer-controlled brain pressure monitoring system. My technical detail blew the competition away and I easily won the contest. The prize was a nice bottle of California Chardonnay. I long ago drank the wine, but I still keep the bottle as a souvenir.

When Expedition Electronics ended, ProLog was waiting with an offer for me to be their northeast Applications Engineer.

That meant I would continue working with Brad and his team, which appealed to me. Brad would remain a fast friend long after my ProLog days, and his insights gave me more than one breakthrough idea as my career progressed. The pay was also great, so I accepted the job. I could finally let go of the stress of running my business and, with the new paycheck, I had the financial stability to buy my very own house for the first time in Jericho and move Eric, Megan, and myself out of our rental house. I felt fantastic as I moved on to my next adventure.

ProLog was a great company, and my kids thought the fact that it managed the rides at Disney World was pretty cool! I was responsible for providing technical support to all of ProLog's East Coast customers, many of whom I had previously tried to serve through Expedition Electronics. I also wrote ProLog's applications notes, and at the annual sales meetings I always won the best technical award, which was kind of fun. I traveled all over the East and Midwest giving seminars. One of the seminars I most enjoyed was the one I delivered in Burlington, Vermont. As I was going through my slides explaining how to design systems using ProLog's components to a roomful of engineers, I was shocked to see Jack enter the back of the darkened room. I continued with my talk, hoping I was impressing him. He told me after the fact that I had!

It was all pretty exciting, and it was at ProLog that I developed my "street smarts" in working effectively with customers to help them achieve their goals, but the job required a lot of travel, and being away from home so much was weighing on me. I felt I wasn't there enough to be a good mom. Eric was in high school and I loved going to his baseball games, and Megan was nine years old with her own sports activities and dancing. I didn't want to miss out on those important experiences while I was flying to Cleveland or Dayton, Ohio to teach engineers how to design the latest and greatest systems. So, after a year of running around the country for ProLog, I called it quits. I needed to get back to a more stable homelife.

When I thought about what I might do next, my mind naturally drifted to IBM, which was still thriving in Vermont near where I lived. I liked the work/life balance IBM had offered, but I knew that IBM had a reputation of refusing to rehire people who had quit. I thought it couldn't hurt to ask, though, and as it turned out, they were having trouble with their test systems and needed me even more than I needed them! And with that, I returned to the IBM fold, with the hope that this time around, I could exert more control over my career and destiny.

Lesson #6 — Pace Yourself to Fit Your Circumstances

I have found there is no shortage of people in the world who are quite happy to tell you what you should do in your life — as a professional, as a parent, as a child, and in any of the million different roles we play in society. As a professional, it is expected that you will continuously advance in a linear fashion and climb the corporate ladder. As a parent, you are expected to shape and guide your children to follow the socially acceptable paths of life. Well-meaning though this advice may be and frequently is, the paths prescribed and encouraged may not always be the best paths for *you*.[1]

You are the only one who knows what is right for you, and it takes maturity and courage to deviate from the norm and follow your own path. It also takes knowing the path you want to pursue. That's not to say that you will have a roadmap with a clearly defined path and landmarks along the way. You may think you do, but life has a way of intervening and knocking you onto different side paths along the way. Knowing the path you want to pursue is less about having a map, and more about having a North Star or set of principles or priorities to guide your steps, whether they are on the path or off. The path from where you are today to where you are headed may be foggy or strewn with obstacles, but as long as you keep your eyes on the North Star—for example, a goal of becoming a CEO, a preference for jobs that directly make the world a better place, a choice to prioritize family over career—then you will be able to find your way forward, even if the path itself is uncertain. Your North Star may change over time as your professional and personal goals evolve, but having a North Star to guide you on the path is critical.

When I made the decision to leave IBM and start Expedition Graphics, it was because I wanted to run a company, and the pathway at IBM seemed to be meandering and less direct than simply running an organization that I started from the ground up. If I hadn't had running a company as my North Star, I might have continued to play the IBM game, and maybe I would have been as successful in my career as I ultimately was, but I'm convinced the decision to try a new path was the right one for me. It was also the right choice for me *at that time*.

The timing was right in my career. I didn't feel I was making significant progress where I was, I wanted to spend more time with my children, and Terry provided the financial safety net I needed in case things didn't work out. All three of those areas aligned at that time to allow me to make the move. If any of those parameters had been different—for example, I felt stimulated by my IBM work, my children were older and less interested in spending time with me, or I didn't have Terry's financial support—I might have and probably would have chosen a different path.

Ecclesiastes 3:1 in the Hebrew Bible (and The Byrds) pointed out that "for everything there is a season, and a time for every matter under heaven." The same principle applies to your career. Your specific circumstances are the backdrop against which your career unfolds. You need to pace yourself to fit those circumstances. Sometimes you should focus like a laser on your career and do all you can to advance. Other times, you will need to fight that urge because taking care of your children or your elderly parents is more important. That's why having a North Star set of principles is so important. They will help you to decide the right path, which may or may not be the path everyone else is encouraging you to take, or even the path that you feel inclined to take.

When I decided to shut down Expedition Electronics, it wasn't an easy decision. I was closing a chapter of four years of my life and admitting that my experiment was no longer working out. Difficult as that decision was, it was the right decision for that time in my life. Things were falling apart with Terry, I was tired of the entrepreneurial treadmill, and the ProLog FAE (field applications engineering) opportunity was the right opportunity for that time period. To the outside world, it might have looked like I was taking a step back from being "chief cook and bottle washer," but you can't be afraid to take a step back or even start over if it is in service to your larger goals. Stepping back at ProLog allowed me to develop and hone my business "street smarts," an extremely valuable skill set that would come into play and continue to evolve over the course of the rest of my career.

Again, ProLog was right for that time period, but *only for that time period*, and so I didn't stay long when I noticed that the excitement of the role didn't make up for what it cost me in terms of time with my children, which again were part of my North Star set of guiding principles. That realization meant potentially returning to IBM, possibly with my tail between my legs. Your life is constantly evolving, so recognize when the pathway is no longer serving your goals, and have the courage to blaze a new trail, even if it may not be so comfortable at first.

Let me close by recalling the maxim that "life is a journey." Trust the journey. My experience and those of just about everyone I know is that the life journey will twist and turn in ways you can't know or even imagine, but that ultimately, if you remain true to your North Star, the end result will similarly be something more wonderful than you could possibly have imagined. Opportunities will come along that you didn't expect. You won't take all of them or even many of them, but the serendipity of life tends to work out for the good. So, stick to your North Star but stay open to the paths that open around you along the way. And enjoy the journey!

Note

1   I am aware of the irony of my saying this in a book containing 12 lessons for life!

Chapter 6

Back to IBM, Again (1985–1990)

As I began to realize that my job at ProLog was having too negative an impact on my personal life, I made up my mind to try to return to IBM and the work/life balance it offered. Knowing that IBM didn't like to rehire people who had quit, my first call was to my old manager, Bob Fiorenza, who had brought me to Vermont in the first place. I knew he would do what he could to get me hired again.

As it turned out, my old tester department in Vermont had replicated my original testers so that there were now five different versions in the lab, but they weren't always working, and no one could figure out what the problems were. Bob made the case that I offered a "critical skill" and should be brought back to get the testers working well again. When he came through with the offer, I was thrilled—I was headed back to IBM with its many benefits and security.

When I stepped back onto IBM's campus, I experienced the same sense of novelty *and* familiarity I felt the last time I returned. I was back in the test department and working on the same testers that I had originally designed, but the department was much bigger now to support the five different types of testers. Also, the "feel" of the office had changed. Thanks to the emergence of email, people were spending more time working in their offices than walking around to speak and work with people in person. That lack of social interaction didn't help me in my re-entry at IBM. I may have gotten the job, but there were a number of people who didn't like the fact that I had returned and saw me as a traitor for having left IBM in the first place.

The test department was no longer a startup with just a few hotshot engineers inventing the technology. It had matured and was now filled mostly with engineers whose job was to keep the variety of testers running. Joe Nelson was one of these engineers, overseeing tester maintenance and power supply, and unfortunately, he didn't like me. He would literally grunt at me when he saw me. He was a lower-level engineer and, in addition to my being a "traitor," I don't think he liked having a young woman above him (even though he didn't report to me).

I could see he had influence in the department, though, and I knew I was going to need to harness the whole team's energy and efforts to achieve what I hoped to accomplish. If I didn't have Joe on board, I wouldn't win over the rest of the team and I wouldn't get much done. So, getting Joe on my side became job number one for me. I turned on the charm, making sure to be friendly to him and offering my help whenever I could, but I was consistently rebuffed. Nothing I tried seemed to work.

Then one day, I was walking past his office when I noticed he had a copy of *Lonesome Dove* by Larry McMurtry on his desk. I popped my head in and asked as casually as I could muster, "Are you reading *Lonesome Dove*? I just read it and loved it." He looked up from his work with an arched eyebrow, as if incredulous that I would be interested in a Western novel. "You've read *Lonesome Dove*?" We started talking about the characters and how marvelously McMurtry had developed them over the course of the book. By the end of that conversation, I felt I had broken the ice with Joe. The next day, I could sense his gruffness softening when I asked about the book again. We talked about the book's colorful descriptions of life in the West, and I knew I was on the way to winning him over when he shared that he was building a cabin on an island on Lake Champlain.

I made it my business to swing by Joe's office every day for the latest updates from his *Lonesome Dove* reading. Joe and I didn't have much common ground on women in the workplace or politics, but we shared a love of the outdoors, Vermont, and *Lonesome Dove*. I built on those commonalities to slowly turn Joe from an antagonist to an advocate. He even ended up inviting Jack and me to his cabin on the island for a visit! And I discovered that once Joe decided he liked you, everyone else quickly got in line.

Joe was prickly and could be difficult, but I was able to appreciate him for who he was. Ultimately, the mission always came first for me, and if I had to occasionally swallow my pride with Joe in those early days to achieve the larger mission, so be it. I focused instead on assessing the strengths and weaknesses of all the members of my teams, figuring out how to best manage them, and aligning them to achieve the mission. I've always found that if you put the mission's success first, your personal success will follow. If you put your personal success (or ego) first, the mission's success is uncertain.

And so, in relatively short order, I had things humming along in IBM's testing department, and before the end of my first year back, Bob and the senior leadership asked me to manage the whole department. I accepted the role, and while it wasn't exciting technically, I ended up really enjoying it.

That promotion also led to my first trip to IBM's management school in Armonk, New York, where new managers were sent for a week of training. IBM had a separate, very impressive campus for management and leadership training. Everyone who attended was assigned a room like a college's dormitory (but much nicer), and the food was absolutely amazing (far better than any college I have visited!).

IBM took the role of management very seriously and trained (and expected) its newly minted managers to be able to handle every situation—from IBM's code of conduct, to managing employees and their performance, to understanding and achieving IBM's business goals and objectives. The school was also a chance for us to meet and network with other new IBM managers from across the United States.

The school ran us through a number of training sessions followed by simulations to see how well we had internalized and acted upon the training. Most of us found the exercises on handling difficult situations to be the most daunting. Those exercises ranged from the more expected—managing an employee having performance problems—to the more socially awkward such as what to do when there are complaints about a team member's body odor. The school was an eye-opening experience and I learned that, upon each promotion, we would be expected to attend another, more in-depth school (so I would have plenty of trips to Armonk in my future).

My first year as a manager was more interesting than I expected and a real game changer for my career. I tore into everything and started to really understand the power of management for the first time. I enjoyed learning how people ticked and how to motivate them to achieve more than they thought was possible. I pushed my people hard and expected a lot out of them, but I always had their back and supported them as they worked to achieve their goals. I remember conducting an annual review for a young engineer on my team and I told him that I thought he had done a good job. He thanked me and told me that it had been a tough year. He said I gave him an incredibly challenging assignment earlier in the year and that he didn't know how to do it. He didn't even think he *could* do it and he was getting demoralized. But he said I never gave up on him and kept pushing him to figure it out, which he finally did. "You helped turn a depressing, demotivating point in my career into a success that made me feel incredible!" Hearing that story made my day and validated my belief that people thrive when you push them to go beyond their self-imposed limits.

But that year also taught me that when you're a manager, it's not about you. When I received the results of IBM's employee engagement survey—my first as a manager—I was thrilled to learn that 100% of my team liked me as their manager (even

Joe!). That felt wonderful to read, but as I read on, I learned that only 30% of my team liked the work our department was doing. *They like me, and they hate their work,* I thought as I realized that what's important is not whether your team likes you. It's about whether they feel their work has meaning and is interesting. If they're not getting that, your management doesn't amount to much and your favorability rating is really just a popularity contest.

After that first year of managing the test group, an opportunity opened for a manager of the design group working on the next generation of IBM AS/400 computer memory cards. Bob encouraged me to take the position as it would also report to him. It was a lateral move and not a particularly exciting position, but product design groups were more prestigious than test design and it would set the stage for my promotion to second-line management two years later, so I accepted the position.

The new role would also begin to take me out of my technological wheelhouse of microprocessors for the first time. My new group included all the card designers whose final products were being tested on my testers, and it was the first time I was introduced to the world of precise design. These products would end up in the offices of IBM's many clients and their performance would be tested in complicated software simulators. For the first time, I had to rely more on the expertise of my team than my own, making it more important for me to assess the talent of the individual engineers who were assigned to me as I couldn't learn and do everything myself.

That year flew by as I learned a ton and put a check in the IBM leadership box, "ability to manage diverse groups with success." I was feeling pretty positive as I checked off those boxes and had a lot of support from upper management, but at this stage of my career, I was simply going where the IBM system led me; I was not yet making my own way. I was competently completing the tasks I was given and reaping the rewards that came with that. So, at the end of that first year, I was offered the opportunity to advance again and become a second-line manager, managing managers for the first time, with three departments and a total of 40–50 people reporting to me. It also came with some nice perks, including a bigger office on the window side of the building and my own administrative assistant.

The group was named "Specials" and covered all of IBM's analog semiconductor components, including drivers, sensors, and radio frequency (RF) chips, as well as the processors that controlled them. Analog technology, which focuses on converting physical phenomena like light, sound, and pressure into electrical and digital signals, was an entirely new area for me. All my experience to date had been focused on digital technology's 1s and 0s and the microprocessors that manipulated them. Being thrust into an entirely new technical area was an interesting challenge and a blessing in terms of further maturing my management skills.

Up until that point, I was still predominantly a *technology-centric* manager. That is, I understood the technology our group was working on as well as, or better than, the rest of the group and leveraged that technical knowledge to manage and advance the group. For the first time, I was now working with a group that knew far more than I did about the technology. I had to become a *people-centric* manager, trusting my people and relying on their knowledge of the technology to move our group forward. My role was less to be the technical expert and more to know how to tap into the skills of the technical experts and motivate them to achieve our goals. I was surprised to discover I enjoyed working with people as much as electrons and realized I could accomplish far more if I trusted my people and delegated the technology's progress rather than trying to do it all myself.

With that promotion, IBM sent me back for another round of management school, but most of my people-management learning occurred "on the job." The new technical conversations were sometimes over my head, and I had to get comfortable with not knowing every detail. I had to figure out who I could trust to give me the straight story, and learn to rely on individuals to get the work done without any technical guidance from me. I also learned that the composition of the team was critical. We needed to have all our bases covered, and it was rare that any one individual could do everything. You had to be careful that you leveraged people's strengths and didn't "put square pegs into round holes."

Fortunately, I inherited three great managers with complementary skill sets. Jim Karl was a whiz with anything process-focused and he managed the manufacturing of our products. Art Adams was brilliant, but also a little wild and crazy in his approach and managed everything by the seat of his pants. Dennis O'Hora was a little older and more seasoned and he was great with managing customer applications. I spent time with them every week, reviewing our opportunities and challenges, learning what made each of them tick, and figuring out the best way to manage them and their teams. I quickly learned that any big technical problems should be given to Art. Quality issues should be managed by Jim, but Jim didn't have the aggressive nature that Art had in solving a thorny problem. Dennis was the guy who handled anything to do with a customer since Art might be too brash and rough around the edges to lead a conversation with an unhappy customer. Together, we were a formidable team.

We also had a lot of fun along the way. In one of our meetings, the guys surprised me by bringing in and arranging on my desk a herd of cows that they had painted brown and labeled with the names of people in our organization. They knew about my farm and cows (more on that in the next chapter), and they laughed that I was managing a second herd at IBM!

Perhaps because I was letting go of the technical reins, I started to be able to manage technology by instinct. Like I said, analog technology was all new to me, but even without understanding its deep inner workings, I began to be able to sense when something technical was amiss, when it wasn't going to work as predicted. I learned how to read my people and know when the technical pieces weren't aligning like they should. I developed the instincts to know when to dive deeper to uncover the problems. This instinctive approach to technology would become increasingly important as I moved up the ladder and gained responsibility for ever broader technology portfolios. For example, when I was the CEO of AMI Semiconductor, my team was working on a new pacemaker/defibrillator device and, even though I wasn't involved with the technology, I had a feeling that the team had not established the appropriate level of quality control and there could be problems. I asked them to add a few extra testing steps and we discovered that there were in fact some problems. By listening to my gut, we likely avoided patients ending up with potentially defective heart devices.

Near the end of my tenure of running the Specials group, I was selected to go to IBM's Assessment School, a school specifically designed to assess leadership talent. Like Officer Candidates School in the military, this school was critical, because it was the pathway to gaining access to IBM's executive echelon. The school was run by instructors, but also by a team of "assessors" who would observe our every move and interaction to determine our executive potential.

So, I made another trip to Armonk, but this time for two weeks. The school placed us in various situations individually and as part of a larger team. My peers were once again drawn from across the United States and were an impressive group. I wondered how I would stack up against stellar colleagues like Bob Mansfield, who would subsequently go on to manage all of Apple's engineering—from MacBooks to iPhones to everything else Apple sold.

Some of the assessment exercises were easy, like sorting through a huge stack of mail and prioritizing responses. Some were more difficult, like simulations in which our team created a business and competed against other teams to see who could deliver the best financial results. I was honored and thrilled when I was asked to present a product and business idea to a group of assessors and I received the highest grades in the class.[1] We were constantly under the microscope at the school. One evening, we went out to dinner at a fancy restaurant with the assessors, and even that was a test. They observed our manners and ability to hold a productive conversation over dinner.

I was pleased that I seemed to be doing very well at the school, but it wasn't all success and accolades. I remember failing miserably one time when I was asked to reject an "employee's" request for vacation time when "a company emergency" arose. The assessor playing the employee pulled out all the stops with a story of how his long-lost grandparents had terminal cancer and had used their last savings to travel from Europe to the US to see their grandson one last time. I struggled tremendously to deliver my bad news and hold my ground.

At the end of the school, I returned to my job energized, excited, and extremely interested to see my final assessment results. When they finally arrived, I was pleased to see that I had done very well. In fact, the assessors' main criticism was that I needed to change my wardrobe! Apparently, my self-made style as one of the few women leaders in the workplace was not quite up to par. I liked my style, but I was always one to take feedback and guidance seriously. Luckily for me, my secretary Leah was a real clothes horse and into fashion. She happily volunteered to take me shopping and we arranged to meet at one of the high-end dress shops in town. When I arrived, Leah already had a ton of clothes waiting for me in the dressing room. I couldn't help but peek at the price tags, which Leah quickly discouraged, but it was too late. Wow! It cost a lot to dress for success. While I couldn't bring myself to buy an entirely new wardrobe at those prices, the pieces she selected for me are still in my closet nearly 40 years later!

As I reflect on my time at IBM's management schools, I'm struck by how amazing, forward-thinking, and rare they were. When I finally left IBM for the last time and became a CEO, I realized that many of my managers and leaders did not have any formal training and did not know how to handle difficult situations. I took it upon myself to design my own training program, traveling the globe to teach my own version of IBM management school to my teams, and the results were always rewarding.

Lesson #7—Success Is a Team Sport

One of the best-known and best-loved of Aesop's Fables is "The Old Man and His Sons" or "The Bundle of Sticks." In this story, a man is upset because his three sons are always bickering and fighting with each other. To help them see the error of their ways, he asks his sons to bring him a tied bundle of slender sticks. The father asks them to break the bundle, which try as they might, none can accomplish. The father unties the bundle, hands the individual sticks to his sons, and asks them to break the individual sticks, which they easily do. The moral of his demonstration is that the sons are stronger when they stand together than when they stand apart as individuals.

In my experience, the same principle applies when it comes to achieving success in business and life. I've known many brilliant people in my career, and I'm fairly smart myself, but none of us is as smart or capable as several of us. Teams have the capacity to accomplish far more than individuals by leveraging the broader scope and power of team members' unique expertise, experience, and perspectives in a concerted effort. It's the concerted effort that determines how successful a team can be.

We've all been part of or seen teams that accomplished far less than would be expected based on the capabilities and potential of the individual members of the team. Aligning and coordinating those individual capabilities is the secret to team success and to achieving far more than any individual can. This principle applies at all stages of your career—at its beginning when you are a junior member of a team and learning and building your network, and in its later stages when you are the one managing people and working to maximize a team's impact.

When I arrived at the testing department, I had big plans. I didn't want to just fix the problems. I wanted to fundamentally improve the performance and potential of the group. But it was one of those situations where you can't do it alone. I would never have had the impact I did if I hadn't focused on aligning and motivating my team to work together to achieve the goals. That team included Joe, who was thoroughly disinclined to work with or even like me, and Joe was one of those people who carried an outsized impact on the team. If he remained out of alignment, the team would never achieve its potential.

Winning Joe over wasn't easy, and it required my being willing to set aside my pride and ego when his gruffness and counterproductive words and actions felt personal (well, I guess they *were* personal). As I mentioned earlier in this book, however, I've always been about the mission. The mission is what most inspires and motivates me, even if it means my ego comes second occasionally. Ego and self-image are not the best guides. If I hadn't been able to take the high road with Joe and continuously seek out pathways to connect with him, I never would have achieved what we did and, ultimately, I never would have been promoted to team manager.

The importance of your team to your success was driven further home when I took over managing IBM's analog semiconductor chips and was no longer the technical lead or "smartest kid in the room." At that point, my technological expertise became less important than my people expertise. I stopped operating as "Chris, the sole proprietor," and started operating as "Chris, the leader of a team of experts and member of something far bigger than herself." That was the start of a more exciting, enjoyable, and rewarding phase of my career. The interesting irony of life is that once we get beyond ourselves, we can achieve far more personal success.

I'm surprised by how often people miss this simple principle or can't rise to the call to set their own egos aside in support of the larger team or mission. I remember helping negotiate the sale of a company whose CEO wanted a benefit after the acquisition that would likely never be needed. This benefit, if it was ever actually needed, would cost such a small fraction of the deal's value that it was the equivalent of a rounding error in the calculation. The CEO of the purchasing company, however, was a cost-cutter and was irritated by the request, so a battle of egos emerged. It became so bad that this very large deal would have fallen apart over a relatively small sum of money if I hadn't set my own ego aside and stepped in to personally guarantee the benefit (which was never needed!). That's what can happen when egos lead the way.

Succumbing to your ego might feel good for a few minutes, but it doesn't really get you anywhere. To achieve maximum success in your life, you need to take a team-oriented and mission-driven approach, even if it means setting aside your ego. This doesn't mean be a doormat. Again, there's a difference between setting your ego aside out of weakness or lack of courage and doing so in support of the team and its larger mission. That difference is results. Setting aside your ego isn't a sacrifice. It's an investment in a future goal. Setting aside your ego is the cost of entry when you're part of a team with a big goal and potentially big results.

It takes a great team to get anything significant done, and the beauty of being a manager and leader is that you have the opportunity to put the right skills together with people you can trust to accomplish more than you ever could on your own. Shoot, I even needed *wardrobe skills* to complete my mission! Or consider my experience as a dairy farmer and showman, which I detail in the next chapter. I knew nothing about these areas, so I had to find the best possible team to help me and rely on them.

Without a strong team, I wouldn't be able to achieve my vision and its full impact. I always worked to put together the very best teams who were loyal and did their utmost to achieve our mission. That was the path to success. Even when the people with the skills I needed did not report to me, I always found a way to entice them to sign on to the mission and work with us to achieve whatever objective was in the bullseye.

I have always loved the saying, "If you want to go fast, go alone. If you want to go far, go together." The truth of that saying has been borne out in my life, time and time again.

Note

1   I smiled to myself, because I found this type of selling much easier than when I sold my caseworker on going to college back in my younger days.

Interlude

The Dairy Farm

In 1985, my adventures as a dairy farmer began. Despite the people-management challenges I was facing at IBM, my job wasn't very demanding overall. I had time and spare brain-cycles on my hands, and that's always dangerous!

That summer, Jack and I went to our local county fair, Addison County Field Days, to watch the tractor pulls. Jack had developed a deep love for tractors while working on a farm in New York from the time he was eight years old until he left home for the Air Force. The big red International Harvester tractors were his favorites. I didn't grow up on a farm, but I found the power and smoke of the tractor pulls to be pretty exciting. As a surprise souvenir from the trip, I bought Jack an International Harvester hat with the red and black emblem on it.

The next year, Jack bought a huge all-wheel-drive 3088 tractor to go with his hat! That summer, we took a week of vacation to see every bit of the Addison County fair and *all* the tractor pulls. Jack loved talking to the machinery dealers during the daytime and seeing the tractor pulls at night. While Jack was talking to the dealers one day, I strolled over to the barns where people were wearing white outfits and showing their cows. I picked up a program and learned that there were six different breeds of dairy cows and each breed would have a champion crowned over the course of the week, and on the last day, the best of the six breeds was named the Supreme Champion of the fair. The prize was a painted portrait of the cow. *It would be really great to win that prize*, I thought to myself. *I wonder if I could figure out how to win that.* I had never touched a cow in my life, and the people who owned and showed the cows had been doing it for generations, but for some reason, the thought of winning that portrait was planted as a seed in my mind that day.

Following that fair we went to Empire Farm Days, which is located south of Syracuse, New York, and is a gigantic machinery show. Once again, Jack was exploring all the tractors and watching the machinery at work in the fields. And once again, I wandered off to check out the rest of the show, and came upon an exhibit of the Brown Swiss Dairy Association. There were three cute calves in a pen who were white as snow and very friendly. I had always loved animals, so when one of the staff came up to me and asked if I would like some literature, I gladly took it. When I opened the booklets, I saw that dairy farming is all about numbers—how much milk, how much fat, how much protein, and all sorts of other production numbers and record keeping. I learned that breeding is all about genetic characteristics and that every trait has a number. As I stood there reading, I thought to myself, *Animals and numbers? What gets better than that?!* I was hooked, and I figured that since Jack loved tractors and always loved going to dairy farms and learning how their operations worked, maybe he would like to be a dairy farmer with me (on the side of course, because we both had jobs at IBM). He humored me, but years later I would discover he liked dairy farming more as a spectator than as a participant! Getting up at 3:30 a.m. every morning to milk cows before going to work gets old pretty fast, and taking out the manure when it is 15 degrees below zero is not fun!

Regardless of the difficulties that no doubt lay ahead of us, I decided right then and there that we were going to start a dairy farm. Of course, we didn't *have* a farm or a cow yet. We just had Jack's big red tractor and my crazy idea. So, I started doing my homework and learned there was a Brown Swiss dairy auction in Cobleskill, New York, in a couple of months. All the Supreme Champions at the Addison County Field Days were Holsteins, which is by far the most prominent dairy breed, but I thought that pursuing the market "white space" with the Brown Swiss breed might be a real opportunity, so I set my mind on acquiring one of them instead. The next problem was how to transport the cow home and where would we put it if we bought one. So, before the auction, we bought a stock trailer and hitched it to our truck prior to setting off for Cobleskill.

I knew we were interested in calves and not a cow that we would have to milk, so I studied the catalogue and breeding beforehand, and we ultimately bought three Brown Swiss calves for $1275. We shortened their registered, formal names to the friendlier Jerry, Vanessa, and Snowy. When we made our winning bids, we still had never touched a cow, but there we were claiming our calves, putting their halters on, and leading them to the trailer. They hopped right in, and we took them home to Vermont.

At that time, we lived in a neighborhood with half-acre lots, but we had a dog pen in the backyard, so that's where the calves went. Between Jack destroying the curbs on our street with his big tractor, and me now keeping three calves in the backyard, our future in that little neighborhood was not looking too bright. We decided we needed a farm! Jack started looking and found a 250-acre farm in Monkton, Vermont, that we could afford. It had an ancient house, but a nice barn, so we bought it and named it Harvester Home Farm. That tractor hat souvenir ended up leading to our starting a dairy farm!

Now that we had a real barn, my mind naturally latched on to the idea that we needed to buy a few more heifer calves to fill it. We ended up buying two more, including one very cute calf named Cassie that Megan immediately took a shine to. Megan was 12 years old and a little embarrassed around her friends that we had cows and a farm, but deep down, she loved them; especially Cassie. She happily toted hay bales, carried buckets, and helped take care of the herd.

Summer was coming, which meant the 1987 fair season would be starting soon. The Addison County Field Days, the fair that had launched my dairy dream, was scheduled for August. It seemed a fitting fair for our first showing of our cows and the results of our efforts. Once I made that decision, I realized how much we needed to do to get ready for our debut.

When I had walked the fair the previous year, I'd noticed how clean the cows and their stalls were. So, to help me prepare for everything that went into a show, I started ordering books about dairy cows and found the 4H Club's books particularly useful. I learned that the heifers needed to be washed and their hair clipped for shows. *Okay*, I thought to myself, *I have my book to guide me. Let's get started washing and clipping.* Little did I know how dirty and sweaty we would get washing and clipping. I spent hours trying to get the clipping just right, going back and forth between the book's pictures and my poor cows.

Eventually, though, we were ready. The calves looked pretty good. From my perspective, they looked *great*! The calves would stay for all five days of the show, and we realized we would need additional on-site support gear, such as a wheelbarrow or something for hauling the manure out of the stalls. So, we ran to a store to buy a kid's orange plastic snow sled (luckily, they were on sale in August!), figuring it was smaller and lighter than a wheelbarrow and would do the job. Finally, we packed up our five calves and gear (including our orange sled) and headed for the show.

We were assigned an area in the large show barn, which housed about 200 animals, and we proceeded to unload our calves and equipment. Most of the families around us who were showing their dairy cows had been doing it for generations. I am sure they had some good laughs at our expense as they watched a couple of yuppies who had no idea what they were doing hauling manure around on a kid's sled. Despite our inexperience, we had fun, and as the public toured the barns, we had a chance to talk and share all we did know with people who knew even less than us! We also met one of our Monkton neighbors at the show; this man had a large farm just down the road from us and was willing to talk to us and share his wisdom, so we peppered him with all sorts of questions—from feeding to breeding.

In the competition, our calves actually won a few ribbons. Megan's calf, Cassie, won first place in her age group! We watched all the old timers showing their milk cows, and as tradition held, the Holstein champion was also the Supreme Champion that year.

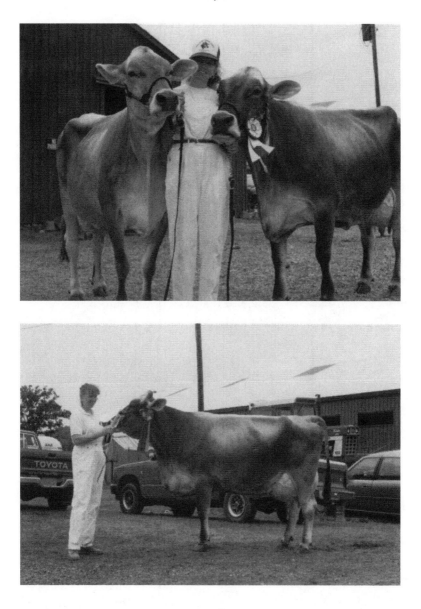

Jack and I had to take vacation time to attend fairs, and Jack couldn't always get away, so Megan and I were on our own when we took our small show-string to the Vermont State Fair. When Megan led Cassie into the show barn, we had to walk past a number of the old timers. We were prepared for some jeering but were pleasantly surprised when one of the men commented, "Nice heifer. She could be the Junior Champion." Megan is just as competitive as I am, and when I turned to look at her, she was beaming. And it turned out he was right—Cassie was named the Junior Champion!

Dairy cows are calved every year to ensure they continue to make milk. So, before too long, we had to learn how to breed our cows. Technology makes it possible for the entire breeding process to be conducted artificially. I loved the challenge of selecting bulls to breed with our heifers. Once again, it all came down to statistics and how the bull might enhance the traits of the heifers in their offspring. We had to buy a semen tank, fill it with the vials from the bulls we had chosen for our heifers, and line up a breeder to come and do the actual breeding.

The trick was to observe when the heifers were in heat and to call the breeder at the right time. I remember one morning I got up at 4:00 a.m. to check for heats, and Jack groggily asked what I was doing since it was still dark out. When I told him I was going to check for cows in heat, he said to me with exasperation in his voice, "Are you really going to breed those heifers? If you do that, we'll have to *milk* those cows!"

"Yes," I fired back. "Isn't that the point?"

I was having fun, but I could tell he was worried that my "fun" was going to lead to a lot of work!

Our heifers became pregnant, and by the next spring, baby calves were on their way. I had never delivered a calf before, so once again the books came out. I read everything I could get my hands on. I knew that once the calves were born, we had to milk our cows—something else I had never done before. Although Jack had worked on a farm, he wasn't much help because he hadn't done much milking either. This time, it seemed to me that milking would be tough to learn from a book, so I had to figure out another way to learn.

There was a very well-run dairy farm not too far away in Shelburne, Vermont, that had a herd of about 80 Brown Swiss cows. They also made cheese from the milk right there on the farm. So, I hopped into my truck and drove to Shelburne Farms. I found the herdsman, a guy named Buster Searles, and told him that I wanted to get a job there. Of course, I had my "day job" at IBM, so I said my working hours would have to be limited to the weekend. He looked at me a little dumbfounded and asked why on earth I would want to moonlight as a dairy hand. I explained to him that we had heifers that were in calf and I needed to learn how to milk, *and fast*! He ended up giving me a job milking the 80 cows in the morning and evening every Saturday and Sunday for minimum wage. And I had to be there by 2:30 a.m.! Everyone probably thought I was crazy, but I thought, *Why not?*

The next Saturday, I got up at 2:00 a.m. and drove to Shelburne Farms in the dark. Buster was already there, and as the cows came into the milking parlor in sets of four, he explained the entire procedure to me. It was all very interesting, but milking cows four at a time meant that it took about three hours to get through the whole herd. The hardest part for me was when I got to the end of the herd and had to milk any sick cows. That involved giving the cows shots of antibiotics and other medications. I hadn't bargained for that. I wasn't big on giving injections.

Buster surprised me that first morning when we finally finished feeding the young calves and all the other chores and he said, "I'll be here tonight and tomorrow, but next weekend you're on your own." I'm sure I looked like a deer in headlights. On my very first day, I was being asked to oversee the whole herd, including dispensing medications. I was a little overwhelmed, but never being one to back down from a challenge, I agreed.

Over the next three months, I spent every weekend at Shelburne Farms. It was a taxing job, but I learned how to milk a cow productively and efficiently. We were ready for our little calves to arrive.

By June we had our first calf; the first of many. One reality of dairy farming is that female calves are worth a lot of money since they will grow into dairy cows. Male calves are worth next to nothing and, just our luck, our first seven calves were all bull calves. We hoped that wasn't an omen of future misfortune as dairy farmers.

The cows often needed help during the birthing process in the form of someone literally pulling the calves out of them, so I would often run home at lunch to check on them. I remember one time I was doing an interview for an *EE Times* article, holding my phone in one hand and pulling a calf out with the other! When my IBM job got more challenging, I would invite my customers to the farm so I could multitask and they could meet the calves and watch the milking process. Sometimes, my colleagues would even come to the fairs to check things out!

Over time, our dairy expertise grew. We continued to buy new young heifers to round out our herd. We figured out who the best cow clipper was in the area, who knew the most about feed, and who was the best vet (and we finally bought some real manure-hauling wheelbarrows!). It was all about learning, watching, and gathering the very best allies we could find. I remember one of our neighbors jokingly complained, "Why are we all helping you?! You're beating us all in the show ring!"

One of the young heifers we bought was named Eliza, and she was a wonderful cow in all ways. She was really big *and* her first calf was a female. In fact, Eliza went on to have six heifer calves. When her milk came in, she had a beautiful udder, which is the primary dairy cow attribute in competitions. Following her first calf, we took Eliza to a small spring show in Vermont. All the old timers and the top cow herdsman could not help but admire Eliza's size, strength, and beautiful udder. The expert Holstein herdsman said she had an udder that could match that of any Holstein. They all called her "the Brown Swiss with the good udder."

Showing a cow that was giving milk was a whole different game from showing a heifer who just had to look clean and pretty. The udders had to look perfect. A dairy udder has four chambers, called "quarters," and each one has to have just the right amount of milk in it for the overall udder to look perfect. The process of getting the right amount of milk into each chamber so that the udder looked full but was not overflowing was quite a feat, and it involved pretty much staying up all night. For example, if the udder needed 12 hours of milk to look good, and the show was scheduled for 2:00 in the afternoon, the cow would need to be milked at 2:00 a.m., and if the quarters were not balanced, each one would have to be milked at different times in the middle of the night!

On the day of Eliza's showing, all I did was stare at her udder, hoping I had milked it at the right time and that it wouldn't overflow. But when she followed me into the show pen, she looked perfect! She was so regal and beautiful, and her perfect udder demonstrated her ability to give a lot of milk. She was crowned the Grand Champion for the Brown Swiss breed. We couldn't believe it! The next class was the Supreme Champion, when Eliza would compete against the Grand Champions of the other five dairy breeds—Holstein, Jersey, Guernsey, Ayrshire, and Milking Shorthorn. My long-held dream of having a cow crowned Supreme Champion was in my sights! As I surveyed our competition, it was clear that it would come down to Eliza and the Holstein. I knew the odds weren't in our favor since a colored cow (i.e., not a Holstein) had never been named the Supreme Champion, but when the judge finally revealed his selection, Eliza had won! The judge actually called out Eliza's beautiful udder in his announcement. I was floating on air!

That was the start of a string of championships for the Harvester Home Farm. The next year, Eliza won the Supreme

Champion for a second time in a row, and her barn mate, Jungle, won Supreme Champion over the next two years. We decided to take our show on the road, all the way to the biggest show in the world in Madison, Wisconsin. Despite the global competition, Jungle was named fourth in the world in her class, and Elegance, Eliza's daughter, won fourth in the world in the heifer class!

We were successful over a period of 12 years in developing a great herd of cows that achieved our goals in the show ring *and* the milking parlor. We had started at the bottom of the heap, without really knowing anything about cows, farming, milking, or showing. So, we read books, we sought out experts, we asked questions, and we listened closely. In my life, Lesson #7, "Success Is a Team Sport," was equally applicable in the world's largest technology companies and on our small dairy farm (and in just about every other area of life). By relying on the wisdom and skills of others and not letting my ego get in the way (which wasn't hard when I was so frequently surrounded by manure), I was able to learn, grow, and achieve tremendous success.

Dairy farming was the ultimate challenge. It was a constant source of hard work and there was never a dull moment. There were endless challenges in feeding, using mechanical equipment, maintaining electrical service, and coping with veterinary problems. Regardless of how we may have felt on any given day, the cows needed to be milked and taken care of twice a day, *every single day*, rain or shine. Looking back, I see that I learned more from milking cows than anything else I have ever done in my life. Dairy-farming results couldn't be hidden or massaged with a nice speech or presentation. The result was simple—how much milk was in the bucket at the end of the day.

Ultimately, however, we had to give up our herd of cows. IBM and executive leadership were calling, but I was sad to let our cows go. When the job at IBM was relatively easy, I could fit the farm in, but as my career took off, it demanded my full-time attention. I comforted myself with the humorous thought that I had probably been the only technology executive who had owned and worked a dairy farm as a hobby!

Chapter 7

Finding My Way (1990–1993)

Things were humming along during the first few years of my management of the analog group. Although there were the normal day-to-day meetings, I had a great set of managers reporting to me and I didn't have to handle many difficult challenges (in fact, it was so easy that I had the time to start my side hobby of dairy farming, which was actually more challenging than my "day job"!). As I went about my daily, weekly, and quarterly tasks, though, I began to wonder what might be next for me at IBM. I knew that "high potential" executives were expected to take an assignment at IBM's headquarters at some point, but I wasn't in any hurry for that and hoped to put it off as long as possible.

Finally, however, I was called into my boss's office. My stomach lurched as I took a seat and he informed me that an assignment had opened up at IBM's US headquarters in Armonk, New York, and that senior-level management wanted me to take the position. I would be on the staff of the new Director of Technology for IBM US, Harry Calhoun. I felt a bit confused as I walked out of his office, not certain if I should be happy that I had been selected or cry because it would mean a big change in my pleasantly steady life. The position was a potentially nice steppingstone for my career, but it wasn't an easy decision to make.

I had returned to IBM precisely because it offered a nice work/life balance, with plenty of time for my family. While the headquarters job would still be with IBM, it was five hours away in Armonk, New York, and my daughter, who was 15 years old at the time, did not want to move to New York (my ex-husband Terry, with whom I shared custody, wasn't a fan of that idea either). I hated having to choose between the future of my career and being a "weekend mother" for my daughter.

After a few weeks of soul searching to determine the best path forward, I came to the realization that my greatest personal gift is being a technology leader. I was good at it; *very* good at it. All my career choices up to this point had been driven by a focus on my role as wife and mother. Family is incredibly important to me, but to turn my back on that future in Armonk would be to waste my gift. For the first time in my life, I recognized that if I didn't take the opportunity, I had reached the plateau at which I would spend the rest of my career. I didn't know what my future would hold if I went to Armonk, but I knew what I *didn't* want it to hold—low-level management positions with low-level impact. It was a hard decision, but I knew I had to go all in and move to IBM's headquarters, hoping that Megan would forgive me for being gone during the weeks.

I planned to commute from our home in Vermont to Armonk every week. I reckoned that if I left very early on Monday mornings, I could be at the headquarters by 9:00 a.m. Since I didn't have any family in New York, I could work late every night and then head back to Vermont in the early afternoon every Friday. I was planning to drive the same blue Chevy pickup truck that I drove to work in Vermont (and that we used on the farm). That plan was nipped in the bud, though, when my boss called me into his office and told me that my truck would not be an acceptable vehicle for someone working at IBM's headquarters. I was amused that rather than giving me advice on how to navigate the cut-throat world of headquarters politics, his primary concern seemed to be that I not take my pickup to Armonk! He encouraged me to go out and buy a nicer car, which seemed silly at the time, but I ended up buying a 1990 Cadillac DeVille. I'm glad I listened to him, though, because when I got to the headquarters, there wasn't a pickup to be seen and my old truck and I would have stuck out like a sore thumb!

I liked my new boss—Harry was new to the job, smart, friendly, and a polished executive—but despite his title of Chief of Technology Strategy, he really didn't know much about the broad spectrum of technology. He was an undisputed process-technology expert, but his new job encompassed all of IBM's technologies, going beyond chip design into systems and software as well. Harry didn't have my experience in those areas. There were a few other people on his team, but none of them were very technical, so he turned to me for just about everything.

Harry and I were both new to the position, and our very first task was to write an overarching corporate instruction document named "CI #101." The manual's contents would govern the quality efforts for every IBM division in the United States, from mainframe computers all the way to the new and burgeoning PC business. The instructions needed to be precise and to the point, and I spent countless hours in my new (and boring!) office laboring over the exact words that would reflect IBM's commitment to technology. When I finally was happy with my messaging, I handed it off to Harry to present to all the division general managers, who were IBM vice presidents. I created a slide deck for Harry to use in the presentation to describe the CI #101 background and how the instructions should be implemented.

As Harry and I walked into the executive conference room for the presentation, I saw that it wasn't a big group, but these were the guys who *ran* IBM. I had heard of most of them but had never met them before. So, I was shocked when Harry suddenly turned to me, shoved the deck into my hands, and said, "Here, Chris. You give the presentation." I am sure my eyes opened wide in surprise, but I took the deck and strode to the front of the room. I was shocked and obviously a little nervous, not just because he had thrown the task at me at the literal last minute, but also because I had never been in front of an audience this senior before. I think the group was also a little shocked to see me up there, but I drew confidence from the fact that you didn't win people over with your position's authority or even the CEO's authority at IBM. You won people over with data, reason, and persuasion. So, I stuck to the facts, and felt my nervousness begin to melt away when I noticed everyone nodding their heads in agreement as I went through the presentation. I knew all the technical details, backing up my proposals with real-world experience, and I didn't falter in my delivery. They were intrigued and very respectful as I gave the presentation. Once the Q&A started, I really came to life and made the new instructions and their potential impact more real for the executives. Harry stood in the back of the room watching with a smile on his face. He was happy the presentation was going so well and seemed to be proud of me.

That was the start of my preparing and delivering just about all of Harry's presentations to the other senior vice presidents on his behalf. I was surprised to be given that opportunity, but I thought it was pretty cool—me, a lowly peon who had only recently moved to the headquarters, interacting with IBM's senior vice presidents on a regular basis! I was no longer working with lower-level managers in my division. I was working with the heads of IBM's divisions, including personal computing, servers, and midrange computers; multibillion-dollar businesses!

Harry gave me other assignments, but none of them were very exciting. One day, however, Harry told me that a task force had been set up to work on IBM's microprocessor strategy. He asked me if I wanted to join it. Of course I did! This was right in my wheelhouse, so I enthusiastically said, "Yes!"

At the first meeting of the group, I noticed there were a lot of smart and experienced people from every IBM division in attendance. As we got into the substance of the meeting, however, I realized that no one was actually in charge and the meeting was starting to meander aimlessly. So, I took that opportunity to step up to guide the group through their thinking. I pulled the relevant people and teams together for weekly meetings, and a coherent strategy began to emerge. Some of the more senior executives would stop by our meetings occasionally to observe our deliberations and make a few comments. One day, Harry called me into his office and told me that Pete Schneider, President of IBM US, had seen me running the meetings. He was amazed and impressed that a young, lower-level woman could keep the group on task and moving in a positive direction. That certainly felt nice to hear!

The days dragged on and, other than the microprocessor meetings, my days were pretty dull. I started to feel like I was stuck in another "do nothing" type of job and began to get bored and restless. It was interesting to be included in strategic discussions about the future of personal computers, especially as Microsoft was getting up and running, but I wasn't actually *doing* anything of substance. I was learning valuable lessons at HQ, getting exposure to IBM's senior executives, and honing my presentation and sales skills, but I really wanted this stint to be over and I *really* wanted to get home to Vermont and my family. These HQ assignments averaged a year in length, but I was sincerely hoping mine would be shorter.

I kept in contact with my friends back at IBM in Vermont, and around the time I was reaching the ten-month mark, there were some rumors of some big, local executive changes. The current site manager, who managed all operations in Vermont and its 13,000 people, was being promoted to a job at IBM's headquarters. As a result, the director who ran the lab, which is where all the design and development happened, would be taking his place as site manager and a new lab director would be named. I was following these moves closely and was elated when I received a call from Hank Geipel, who was being named the new lab director. He asked me if I would like to manage his staff. The title would be Chief of Staff, IBM Burlington Laboratory. I was thrilled by how much more exciting this job would be and I didn't have to think for even a nanosecond.

Things moved quickly and I was back in Vermont in less than a week. The Chief of Staff position was exactly the kind of substantive job I wanted—a second-line management position where I was responsible for the technical plan for the site as well as the overall financial performance. I was also in charge of patents and technical education and programs. There were 2,000 people working in the lab, and those teams designed all the chips that the site manufactured. As I walked into my new office, I noticed that it was a busy place and that the prior Chief of Staff had left piles of phone messages stacked up everywhere. Rather than being overwhelmed, I was motivated by how much more stimulating this job would be than my previous job at headquarters. My office was around the corner from a luxurious office suite where Hank and his secretaries sat. Hank expected me to be in his office at 7:30 every morning, and we usually worked until well past dinner, but I loved it.

As much as I enjoyed sinking my teeth into a real job again, it came with some tasks that wouldn't make me particularly popular with the other executives at the lab. There were two huge programs in development at the site that were focused on IBM's next generation of memory chips. No one had ever manufactured memory chips at this density before. As such, the challenge wasn't just the design of the chips. It included constructing the new manufacturing lines to build the chips. This all cost a lot of money. In fact, we were only a few months into the year and the lab was already running seriously in the red.

Hank was responsible for all of this, so it was up to me to keep everyone's spending in check. As these two big programs were critical, I had to make sure everyone else at the site reduced their spending, which didn't make me popular. I had to keep an iron fist on the budgetary policies and expenditures of Hank's managers and their subordinates, all of whom were senior to me. Thanks to my role, everyone was exceptionally nice to me since I controlled their purse strings, but they also hated to see me coming.

It wasn't an easy role, but I hunkered down, continued to make the tough decisions, and succeeded in getting the site back on financial track. My moment of affirmation and fame finally arrived when our Division General Manager, Mike Attardo, who oversaw 50,000 people, came from the headquarters for his monthly review of our businesses. I was tapped to present our financial status to Mike since I had done such a good job of managing the budgets and the results had started to reflect my efforts. I gave Mike a succinct review of our status and committed that we would stay on budget for the rest of the year. I could tell that Mike wasn't used to having a woman present to him. Of course, how could he be? I was still the only woman at IBM in Vermont at my level! I could also tell that Mike was very happy with the results. As I wrapped up my presentation, Mike said, "Keep up the great work! I'll see you next month."

I found that working for Hank was interesting. He had a PhD in engineering and was very smart and successful, but he seemed to struggle with work/life balance (for himself and all of us!). He was all about the job and very dictatorial—it was his way or the highway. I remember a funny conversation we had after we returned to the office following a long Memorial Day weekend. I asked Hank if he had had a good weekend, and he responded sternly, "No!" He said his family never did what he told them to do. I think he preferred to be in the office where he had 2,000 people at his beck and call. If you had told me then that Hank would one day report to *me*, I wouldn't have believed you.

Despite Hank's gruff manner, I finally won his loyalty. Hank had to present his annual plan every year to the site manager.

We had stacks of slides with tremendous numbers of financial graphs on them. When Hank was presenting this time, it became clear that he had made an incorrect assumption about the financial projections for the memory business, and I could see he was in trouble with his boss. As he was trying to backtrack and spin a story to explain why the assumption was incorrect, I quickly blurted out, "I think I made a mistake when I made the charts." The site manager took my confession in stride and smiled at Hank — the confrontation was over. On our way back down the stairs to our suite of offices, Hank thanked me for what I had done. It was the only mention of what had happened, and we moved on to bigger and better things.

On the family side, it was nice to be back home, but my job was increasingly becoming a 24/7 deal. Megan was 16, in the middle of her formative teen years, and I felt guilty about how little I was seeing her. I spoke with Megan and asked if she wanted to come to the office with me when I was working on nights and weekends, to which she replied, "Yes!"

So, we started "working" together. While I did my work, I let Megan play around on our computers with the early presentation program FreeLance. She asked what we did with FreeLance, so one of my managers handed her a hand-scribbled chart and explained that we used the program to make the chart look professional. Twenty minutes later, Megan handed us a beautiful FreeLance chart which was a perfect but more stunning replica of the original. We couldn't believe it! Almost immediately, there was a line of people waiting to give Megan their charts so she could work her "magic"! Although she was only 16 years old, she became a respected member of the team and soon became indispensable. It was quite a "bring your child to work" experience for her (and me!). Megan started coming to work after hours, helping my team with the charts for their presentations detailing the plan for the whole laboratory — and she loved it, but my staff loved it more!

As the one-year anniversary of my managing the lab staff came around, I wondered how long I would stay in the position. The Chief of Staff role was considered another "learning" job, and I certainly got to see how a high-level executive operates (although I wasn't sure Hank's dictatorial management style was something I wanted to emulate). I had a chance to work on a few interesting projects, such as closing an IBM contract with Apple to put IBM's PowerPC microprocessor into all of Apple's computers[1] (it was eye-opening to witness how Steve Jobs operated). By the end of the year, we were back on budget, and my "make friends with everyone" approach meant that none of the senior executives had stabbed me in the back. Hank was happy with my planning and attention to detail, and my regular meetings with our division chief, Dr. Attardo, had gone extremely well.

So, one morning at our daily 7:30 meeting, Hank informed me that there was another reorganization coming and that it was time for me to move on. He said there was a third-line management spot for me. I was happy to be offered my first third-line management role, but I was also a little uncertain. I would be the leader of the Application Specific Integrated Circuit (ASIC) group and I didn't have a lot of experience with this type of technology. ASICs are custom chips tailored to a specific application, which in this case were IBM midrange computers. I would have three second-line managers reporting to me, and my group would be about 100 engineers and technicians strong. I took the position, which was the greatest level of responsibility I had held so far in my IBM career.

On my first day in the job, I arrived at my new, even bigger office. My secretary was once again the stylish and ever-competent Leah, and I arranged to meet with each of my managers — Tim, Jim, and Jeff. By the end of that first day, though, I had the distinct feeling I would have to do a lot to win these guys over. First of all, they were all very smart and technical and they had had this realm to themselves for a number of years. Also, I was the one who had been scrutinizing their budgets for the last year, and they weren't happy about the decisions I had made. Finally, I got the impression that they thought I had been promoted only because I was a woman or because I had spent time at headquarters. They were passive-aggressive in nearly every interaction, and I could see they would be a challenge to manage. I realized that this was going to be a lot harder than getting Joe Nelson to respect and collaborate with me (I didn't see a *Lonesome Dove* moment coming in the near future).

My boss was Ken Torino, who had also been my boss when I worked in the "Specials" analog group. Ken was a pretty nerdy guy and had a tight relationship with my three managers. My trio of managers often went around me and directly to Ken when they needed something, but I kept trying to figure out how I could become their respected leader and add value to their personal careers. Part of my management philosophy has always been to figure out how to provide personal value to those I manage by making them more successful financially and in their careers. While I was working to figure that out, though, I focused on learning and understanding our internal customers in the other divisions of IBM.

About six months into the role, in early 1993, I was starting to hit my stride and then, one day, Ken called me into his office.

"Chris," he said, "IBM has traditionally targeted having seven layers of management, but over recent years that number has crept up. Leadership has made the decision to reduce the number of layers again by expanding managers' spans of control, and unfortunately, your job is being removed..."[2]

I was shocked. Well, it made sense, because Ken didn't seem to have much responsibility and taking over my group would help alleviate that, but I didn't see anyone else having their management positions taken away and I felt like I'd been punched in the stomach.

I left that meeting on the verge of tears. It had taken me so long to become a higher-level manager and I felt that I had done everything right to get there—from expanding my technical and managerial skills to successfully navigating an exceedingly challenging political environment. Now, they were removing me from management and, while I wasn't being laid off, they didn't yet have another job planned for me. I was adrift, and crushed by the setback. Over the next day or two, I wallowed in self-pity and did my share of crying, wondering if this was the end of my career at IBM. I couldn't see any clear path forward.

In adverse situations, though, my instinct is to "think outside the box," and that's when I tend to make my biggest jumps. I decided to stop moping about, take control of my destiny, and *do* something about my situation. While I had previously been happy to let the IBM career system sweep me along with whatever their plan was for me, it certainly wasn't working anymore. I needed to take control of the situation.

Maybe there would be a place for me at IBM and maybe there wouldn't be. I needed to broaden my skills so that if there wasn't an opportunity for me any longer at IBM, I could find a job somewhere else. We had been highly successful in designing IBM's technology and had invented and developed some amazing processes and products, but it was a slow process, expensive, and unfortunately proprietary and non-transferable. And even if you wanted to use our chips in products developed by companies outside IBM, it was virtually impossible thanks to IBM's crazy, non-commercial standards. I decided I needed to use whatever time I had left at IBM to expand my knowledge and skill set to include an understanding of how other people in the semiconductor industry designed chips.

Coincidentally, IBM was struggling at the time. John Akers, the Chairman and CEO of IBM, was rumored to be out, and there was talk circulating that IBM could be broken up into pieces. While those machinations were far above my level in the corporate ether, I could sense that my division, now called IBM Microelectronics, was also a little desperate. Our division had always been focused on serving IBM's internal customers with its memory and PowerPC microprocessor products, but we had just consummated the Apple deal for the PowerPC to be the engine of all future Apple computers. Following that success and an industry-wide shortage of memory devices, I heard IBM was considering selling its chips to customers outside IBM.

At that time, most of the IBM executives were focused on the successful memory (DRAM) and PowerPC businesses where IBM was taking on Intel. I realized that the ASIC business I had been managing was an untapped opportunity that no one was focused on. The ASIC market was hot. IBM's ASIC research team had delivered some stunning innovations, but again, they were limited to IBM's use. We were sitting on a gold mine if I could connect the market with our supply.

I realized I could start a business taking IBM's great ASIC technology to other big, external customers, and even if IBM never got around to successfully selling their chips externally, the experience would give me exposure to new chip-design processes and other companies where I might be able to find a job if things didn't work out at IBM. I could hit two birds with one stone. Either IBM would work out, or I would learn enough to get a job somewhere else. Win-win!

With nothing really to lose, I went back to Ken two days after he let me know my job was going away and asked him to give me a small team of about 15 people that I could turn into applications engineers able to talk to customers about using and applying our technology. I explained my vision of using that team to create a business selling ASICs to customers outside IBM. It wasn't an awfully hard sell—I didn't even have to explain *how* I would do it (which was a good thing because I didn't know yet!). My request solved Ken's problem of what to do with me now that I no longer had my third-line manager position. The ASIC group wasn't a business on people's radar screens since it had no external customer base and was smaller than the memory and PowerPC businesses. He probably figured I wouldn't be able to do much damage to or with it! For Ken, it was the perfect solution to his "Chris problem." For me, it was a lesson in not waiting for other people to solve my problem. I shudder to think about where I would have ended up if I had waited for Ken to find a new position for me. As it turned out, my initiative to chart my own future accelerated my career in ways I never could have imagined.

Ken gave me a handful of smart people and access to some great technology, but no budget, no existing market or customers, and no business processes. And no attention from the IBM "powers that be."

No problem, I smiled to myself as I began blazing my own path at IBM for the first time.

Lesson #8—Think Boldly and Out of the Box

One of my favorite parts in a book or movie is when the protagonist has a moment of enlightenment when they are shocked to realize that the situation is not at all what they expected. The path they are following is not going where they thought it would. The person they thought was their ally turns out to be an adversary (or vice versa). I enjoy that moment because it marks a turning point where they are able to see more clearly the reality they face and can take a wiser path in the future.

I described my meeting with Ken when I learned my job was being eliminated as being like a punch in the stomach. It was completely unexpected. I had done everything that had been asked of me, everything that was expected of me, and I had exceeded their expectations. And yet, in that meeting, I learned that the path that had been laid out for me and the progress

I had made was little more than a façade. That meeting was a gut punch, but it knocked me out of complacency and provided the moment of clarity and the catalyst I needed to realize that it was time to take control of my own destiny and begin walking my own path.

"Thinking outside the box" is the call to eschew the tried and true in favor of exploring and pursuing new, potentially better paths. That phrase is used so often in the corporate world that it has become a parodied cliché, but I still like it, if only as a call to arms to not just settle for the status quo. The real challenge, though, is *seeing* the box. We are all in our own boxes—on the small scale in our day-to-day operations, but also on the large scale in our lives. We are busy with our life plans and carrying them out, and "the box" is our entire worldview and the backdrop against which our lives are played out. Since we are "in" the box, we struggle to see it.

Adversity, then, is like a pair of glasses that helps us to see more clearly. It can reveal the box. No one likes going through adversity, but all of us do. Not to discount the trauma that some people must labor under day upon day, I do think that for most of us, adversity can be cathartic. It can be clarifying as the trivial is scraped away by the sandpaper of life and we can see our situation, what matters, and the path forward more clearly. Every moment of real adversity in my life has led to greater clarity and served as the catalyst to spur me on to greater achievement than I had ever thought possible before.

Whether you have the benefit of adversity or not, I encourage you to see your box. Look for the corners and edges that show the limits of your thinking, opportunity, and experience. If you're doing the same thing day after day on a path that is uninspiring to you, it's a good bet you're operating in the box. If you're not learning something new and expanding your horizons every day, you're in the box. If you're not being challenged or challenging yourself, well, you get my point.

Once you can see your box, though, how do you "think outside" it? How do you spot the opportunities for something greater than your current situation? Looking for the three-way intersection of the white spaces I described in Chapter 4, your core competencies, and the adjacent emerging or potential skills you possess, is what has worked for me. Matching your core competencies to white-space opportunities facilitates success. That is, a white space may exist, but if you have no competencies to address it, you will fail. And looking for opportunities that leverage and strengthen your nascent skill sets facilitates personal growth and the emergence of additional opportunities in the future.

When I pondered my situation and looked for a way out of my box, I realized three things. First, IBM was creating new white space by considering the sale of its components to external customers for the first time, and while the memory and PowerPC white spaces were likely to fill in quickly, the ASIC space was wide open. Second, I realized that my expertise, experience, and current position gave me the critical skills I needed to pursue that opportunity and own that white space. And finally, I had been thinking about using external components in IBM systems and selling IBM components to external customers for years. Liaising successfully between IBM and the external market wasn't my core competency, but it was something that I felt I could build and strengthen with practice. Creating a new IBM business selling ASICs to external customers hit all three metrics for a good "outside the box" path forward for me.

Knowing what to do and *doing it* are two different things, however. It takes courage to operate outside the box. When I went to Ken with my idea of launching an entirely new business, I had the benefit of having nothing really to lose. I already didn't have a job, and even if selling ASICs to external customers didn't work out, at least I would have learned something that

I could use to find my next position. There were no guarantees I would be successful. In fact, the odds weren't exactly in my favor. The secret to success is not waiting until the outcome is certain, because it will never be, or by the time the outcome is certain, everyone else will already be crowding your previous "white space." I didn't even know what success would look like! I wasn't aiming to build a billion-dollar business. I was just doing something I thought I would learn from and *maybe* find success. The secret is just getting started and figuring it out as you go along. There will be bumps and zigs and zags along the way, but my experience is that if you focus on doing the right thing for the right reasons, it will work out. If you do the best you can, life tends to work out.

Notes

1   Up until that point, my division, IBM Microelectronics, had developed and manufactured parts only for other IBM divisions.
2   As it turned out, mine was the only job being eliminated. I never found out the reason why, but maybe it was just that they knew I wouldn't make a fuss.

Chapter 8

Into the Stratosphere (1993–1997)

Per my usual "just get started and figure it out as you go along" approach to my career and life in general, I signed up to build our external ASIC business without knowing how I was going to do it. What I *did* know, however, was how to attract and align people who could help me do it. I started with the little group of ASIC engineers who had initially joined me.

The ASIC group at IBM Burlington developed basic technology for the divisions across IBM that designed computers and the chips that went into them. Our engineers were exceedingly smart, but I was asking them to take on tasks they had never attempted before. Not only had they not designed chips in the non-IBM world before, *they had never designed any chips whatsoever*—our IBM customers did that! We had a lot to learn! But I figured that the group was strong and the knowledge and skills we currently lacked could be addressed with focus and time. Plus, I knew that we had the most innovative foundational technology in the business. I just needed to figure out what customers outside IBM actually wanted and point our engineering team in that direction.

My first step was to meet some customers. The problem was that I didn't *have* any customers other than IBM and didn't really have any idea about what customers outside IBM were doing. So, I reached out to my friend Brad Paul (from my Expedition Electronics and ProLog days), and he was happy to help me find some small semiconductor design houses in the New England area that had strong engineering teams with whom I could test out our nascent ASIC strategy. Before we hit the road, I huddled with my newly minted IBM applications engineers to create a presentation deck that described our technology and how it could be used by external customers. With that in hand, I jumped in my car and headed to Boston to meet up with Brad. It was fun to be on the road with him again, going out to call on customers with, in my opinion, the most bad-ass technology on the planet!

I spent the next few weeks presenting to potential customers and absorbing their feedback like a sponge. My presentation went over quite well. The customer engineers oohed and aahed over the speed and density of IBM's technology. As I went through my deck, I closely watched the facial expressions of the people in my audiences to get a sense of times when they didn't quite understand, or worse, didn't believe what I was saying. For example, one of the questions I received was how short the delay was across IBM's circuits, and when I took a guess, answering, "Two picoseconds," some of the engineers rolled their eyes. *Ooof*, I thought to myself. *I flubbed that answer.* When I debriefed with my team later, I learned the actual answer was 200 picoseconds, which was still great, but I understood why the engineers had rolled their eyes when I gave an answer that was two orders of magnitude faster than what we could actually deliver. There were also questions that stumped me about how the design process worked, since IBM designed in its own proprietary environment and I wasn't sure how things would work outside that environment. I would have to figure that out!

Overall, however, our "test customers" were very impressed with what IBM had to offer and I returned to my office in Vermont invigorated. I immediately gathered my small group of engineers together to share what I had learned (they all had a good laugh when I shared my "two picoseconds" answer). Everyone was excited to hear the customers' reactions and bubbled over with ideas on how to improve our pitch. They could start to see the potential that I had been talking about. We were all on a steep learning curve, but it was clear there was a large market to be captured if we executed well, and my team was eager to dive into the work necessary to create a viable product for customers.

First, I needed to recruit some real chip designers. My fledgling IBM group knew how to design the component pieces of a chip, but not how to put them together in a full, integrated chip. When Brad and I had been driving between customers on our tour, I had confided to him about my staffing challenge and, as always, he had a great solution—hire some subcontractors to seed and grow our expertise. Brad connected me to a chip-design company in Boston, who connected me to another company in Silicon Valley. I was able to hire four subcontractors from those design houses to get my group up and running.

Little did I know as I was getting them their badges on their first day that they would go on to radically change IBM's future with the expertise and experience they injected into our group. They became key members of our team and provided much-needed leadership in those early days. Coming from outside IBM's staid culture, their dress code of T-shirts and sneakers was a bit of a shock, but their technical excellence made their style divergence quickly fade in importance. This was just a taste of what was to come—when I started bringing external customers to IBM, especially from Silicon Valley, some of them showed up in sandals!

All of our efforts would be for nothing, though, if we didn't secure some budget to fund our work. As it turned out, the "budget angels" smiled on us and I received a phone call from our headquarters that Unisys, a major midrange computer supplier, wanted to speak to someone about access to IBM's semiconductor technology. Unisys had always manufactured their own semiconductors, but apparently, they were thinking of outsourcing that task to someone else, which would be a big move for them. The staffer on the other end of the line asked if I would meet with them. "You bet I will," I said back into the phone, scarcely believing my luck.

I scheduled a meeting with the head of the semiconductor division of Unisys, Dick Joy, and from our first meeting it was clear that he was excited about what we could do for them. While Unisys still wanted to design their own chips, they didn't have access to the technology and methodology to bring them to market—but we did. Since everything was brand new, when it was time to put a price on our capabilities and services, I was not shy. I put a price on everything, from access to technology libraries to various software packages, and began sending out multimillion-dollar invoices—and they paid them! I couldn't believe it, but my team could finally get to work!

Dick told his CEO that IBM would be providing their chips in the future, and suddenly, our little project became a strategic focus of the Unisys senior executives. They requested a meeting with our division head Mike Attardo, Jim Picciano (the head of IBM's semiconductor division), and other IBM senior executives. When IBM set up the meeting, they really didn't know what the meeting was about and left me off the invite list, but when Dick saw I wasn't included, he specifically requested that I attend. It was a good thing he did that because, again, our IBM senior executives really didn't have any idea what the meeting was about or what I was doing!

We were going to meet at the Unisys headquarters in Bluebell, Pennsylvania, which meant I got to take my first helicopter ride to get there. I felt pretty important riding in a Sikorsky helicopter with the top executives from my division. The helicopter was so loud that we all had to wear headphones, making conversation impossible, which was fine with me since I wouldn't have known what to say to those guys.

At the meeting, all the senior executives were seated around the table, and as the most junior person in the room, I sat in the back against the wall. Then, the Unisys CEO asked to speak with the person "who is doing all the work," and Dick pointed to me. I stepped forward and found myself addressing the senior leadership of Unisys while IBM's senior executives looked on a little dumbfounded. They were probably wondering who this Chris King was and why the CEO of Unisys wanted to speak with her. At the end of our meeting, the CEO turned to me and said, "It's up to you, Chris, and we're counting on you to make this successful." You could have knocked my bosses over with a feather. They were surprised that they had no idea what was going on in our group. Ken had not been paying attention to what I was doing and had not kept his managers informed. They realized, though, that I was on to something and that they needed to support me. That's when Mike, who already knew me from my lab-budgeting days, and Jim Picciano started paying attention to our group. A few months later, Jim presented me with my first IBM stock grant as a result of the Unisys deal, letting me know that none of my immediate managers had stock grants. I was floating on air. The Unisys deal gave my group revenue, budget, visibility, and credibility.

With our learnings from those early presentations and our experience and revenue selling to Unisys, our presentations continued to get better. We realized we were ready to "hit the road" and start aggressively pursuing more customers. There was a young engineer newly out of school, Brendon McGuire, who had been working in Boston as a salesman before he moved to IBM Microelectronics in Vermont on a whim because "it looked interesting." Brendon wasn't in my group, but he was the type of person that people naturally want to buy from, so I "borrowed" Brendon from his current group to cold call customers like HP, Sun Microsystems, and Apple. One nice thing about calling from IBM is that *everyone* wants to talk to you. At the very least they wanted to know what "Big Blue" was working on.

Finally, Brendon and I hit the road. Many of the companies we met had been doing their own designs like Unisys, but just about everyone was very interested in the possibility of switching over to IBM technology in their products. It was great technology, after all. We were making sales almost from day one, and I remember sitting in my hotel room writing product-shipping instructions in the dead of night because no one had ever sent parts outside IBM before!

One of our first sales was to Qualcomm for its first CDMA-based mobile phone chip (which ushered in the era of cell phones without external antennae). I actually got into trouble for selling to Qualcomm because my managers thought I was wasting my time chasing "unsuccessful startups." At the time, Qualcomm was mostly known for tracking freight and trucking, and my managers didn't recognize that Qualcomm was targeting an entirely new market or that it would grow to be one of our largest customers! In fact, Qualcomm would grow into a technology powerhouse and ultimately provide components for almost every mobile phone in the world.

At that point, we were just providing base technology and manufacturing support for chips that were predominantly designed by our customers. That changed when we started working with Cray, the supercomputer manufacturer. Cray had been working unsuccessfully with Motorola on the design of an incredibly complex set of chips. In frustration, Cray reached out to me to see if IBM could help, and I was able to convince them to drop Motorola and take a risk on my little group for end-to-end support of their chips' design, including our design methodology, software, and libraries (the subcomponents of the chips)!

To achieve what I was promising, though, I would need to rapidly scale up my team. Fortunately (for me at least), IBM was in the process of shutting down a few computer-design sites, so I took advantage of the closure of the site in Kingston, New York, to hire 25 of its design engineers who knew how to design higher-level ASICs (up until that point, with the exception of my for-hire subcontractors, we were only designing *components* of the ASICs like gates and libraries). I finally had a full team of engineers who were experts in designing chips.

And then I lucked into Ann Rincon. Ann was a whiz engineer who didn't want to be forced into a management path. Her exact words when we met were, "I don't want to have to babysit whiny engineers." IBM, like most companies, promoted engineers who were good at what they did to positions of management, which is an entirely different skill set and career path. Ann was feeling pressure to enter that management track, so she came to speak with me, and we made a deal—she would come work for me and I would never make her have to be a manager. It was a good move for both of us. Ann would end up winning the *Electronic Design Automation* Marie R. Pistilli Women in Engineering Achievement Award in 2002 for her work on our project, and it was the beginning of a long and wonderful professional relationship together. Ann would later work for me at AMI Semiconductor and SMSC, where I was CEO, and Cirrus Logic, where I was a member of the Board of Directors.

I put Ann in charge of the design system that customers would use to design their own chips using IBM technology. We started out by trying to emulate the design processes of our competitors LSI Logic and VLSI Logic, the leading design companies at the time and the behemoths of the ASIC market, but integrating IBM technology within their processes and qualifying them was taking too long for our customers' needs. Once again, Brad Paul came to my rescue. I was complaining to him about our challenges copying LSI's and VLSI's processes, and he wisely asked how IBM designed its own chips. "IBM has great computers. You must be doing something right." His idea was that we should get everyone to design chips the way we had always done it at IBM, instead of trying to design our chips the way the industry leaders and our competitors did. He was right. Ann and I realized we could use a streamlined timing simulator and automated test patterns, as we did at IBM, to help our customers get to market faster and more easily than they would if they used the traditional LSI or VLSI "golden simulator" process. Ann and I got in a room and started working on a new design system based on "the IBM way." Then, I created yet another set of slides to explain it and sell our customers on a whole new way to design their chips.

I took the new design process to Apple in Cupertino, California, explaining that we would cut out the onerous golden simulator step and give them the two IBM tools free of charge to automate their design process. They loved that! Ultimately, our design process and tools became the way *everyone* in the industry designed semiconductor chips, and they remain the industry standard today!

Things had really started cooking for our group—we were growing, had customers, and were starting to churn out designs—but we still had a way to go before we could deliver a complete chip for our customers. I knew I would need to continue leveraging the resources of our division and, importantly, circuit engineers, packaging engineers, software experts, manufacturing staff, and other employees from other divisions that didn't report to me to deliver the complex systems our customers wanted. So, whenever a big customer like HP came in to discuss their needs, we would gather people from across IBM Vermont and its widely disparate organizations to meet with them. I was not their manager, but the allure of meeting with a "real" customer like HP, Apple, or Cray was irresistible (plus, I always brought great snacks to the meetings!). We would all get together in a large room, with the customer team on one side of the table, IBM's various engineers on the other side, and me in the middle orchestrating the discussion and bringing the two teams to consensus and commitment.

Those Cray chips were the first chips that we designed using *all* of our capabilities. We brought together new lithography technology (the process by which computer chips are built up), new packaging (the package in which integrated chips are housed and made usable), new design methodology, new everything! When the first chips rolled out, more than 90% worked perfectly and we were able to correct the problems with the remaining chips in a day. Cray said it was the fastest successful chip production in their history. Cray was our team's first significant success. And other customers quickly followed—HP, Apple, Teradyne, Ericsson, Silicon Graphics, Alcatel, and on and on. HP's medical division was building a new ultrasound system, and we would go on to help them create the first million-gate ASIC!

I would visit *any* customer in those days (and we had now grown to the point where we had actual sales reps). One time, I went to visit a startup networking company named Juniper that had fewer than 20 employees and was operating in an office in a strip mall. I presented our capabilities and they liked what they heard. And I was impressed by them. They were smart, capable, and hungry. Once we started working with Juniper, however, Cisco, which hadn't given me the time of day before, asked to meet with us. Cisco was the holy grail of the ASIC industry and they were an LSI Logic customer, so winning them would be huge for my team. I invited them to one of my marathon brainstorming meetings in Burlington and they were impressed by our team and its capabilities. At the end of the meeting, I asked them, "What else can I do for you?" and without hesitation they responded, "Please don't work with Juniper." I tried not to smile as I thought to myself, *Bingo! We've got Cisco!* Ultimately, we ended up working with *both* Juniper (the hungry startup) *and* Cisco (the company that would become our largest customer).

While our team started to notch these additional wins and grow, I was busy navigating IBM's management team. As I mentioned earlier, the higher levels of management weren't really paying attention to me and the ASIC business at the start.

But then Lou Gerstner came on board as the new CEO of IBM in 1993. He was mocked as the "cookie guy" since he came to IBM from Nabisco, but I've learned that outside perspectives can often generate the greatest impact in an organization and Lou had the best technical instincts of anyone I ever met. In fact, he is one of the best *leaders* I ever met—maybe *the* best—and I learned more from Lou than anyone else in my career.

One of Lou's management mantras was to talk to customers every day. He asked our General Manager, Mike Attardo, to provide updates on our division's customers, which wasn't easy. Mike turned to his staff: "How am I going to report on customers? I only have *one* [IBM]!"

Someone piped up, "That King woman might have some customers."

Mike had a division of about 50,000 people and I was just a lowly manager, so my secretary and I were shocked to get a call from his office. He asked if I had external customers and I said yes and began to rattle off a list—Unisys, Cray, and so on. Mike asked if he could "go on the road" with me to meet our customers, which I thought was pretty cool! Calls from Mike became a regular thing, and my secretary Leah took great pleasure in calling out to me loudly so everyone could hear, "Chris, Dr. Attardo is on the phone for you." I enjoyed rides with Mike in private jets and limousines and the extended one-on-one time with "the boss" in my natural element—working with customers. Those visits impressed Mike, both in terms of my abilities and what I was doing.

Later, we learned that Lou Gerstner would be coming to visit our division in Burlington, Vermont, and each group was going to present to him. At the time, my manager Ken was on vacation, so I was asked to prepare for and provide the briefing. Since I knew that Lou liked to talk to customers, I decided to invite some of my customers to present to him. I invited HP's medical division and their ultrasound team, whom we had worked with on the first million-gate ASIC, and the Qualcomm team with their new phone demo. I wrote all of this up in the preparatory briefing documents, but my management team didn't pay attention until the night before Lou's visit. All the other groups had very techy presentations focused on our products—PowerPC, memory chips, and so on—and when the management team read my briefing, they realized that I was bringing in customers whose comments could not be managed or controlled, and they were pretty upset with me. I received a visit from John Gleason, the new head of sales for IBM Microelectronics, at 7:00 a.m. on the morning Lou was coming in and was told in no uncertain terms that I had better control the conversations with my customers or there would be trouble.

When Lou came through and got to my demo of our ASIC products, I could see that the technology bored him almost immediately and I knew I had made the right choice about bringing in my customers. When I introduced him to HP and Qualcomm, his eyes immediately lit up! The HP guy used his ultrasound machine to show Lou his gallbladder, which fascinated him. Then Qualcomm showed him a phone that didn't contain the standard visible antenna thanks to our chip. Lou ended up spending more time at our demo than any other in our division (his staff actually had to drag him away!). Later, when Lou addressed the site's thousand managers, he said, "When your wife says you are good-looking it's one thing, but when your wife's friend says it, it's a whole different level of compliment. I spoke with some of our competitors today and they say our technology is great! Now *that's* saying something." I was blown away because I knew he was talking about the customers that I had brought. I heard later that on the way to the airport, Lou said to our site manager, "Take care of that King woman. Customers like her."

In a high-level management meeting later that month, Mike Attardo remarked, "Whoever had the idea to introduce Lou to our customers was a genius!" By then, of course, I think they had forgotten that it was me.

I was starting to realize the full power of the customer. It was a customer (Unisys) that gave my little team and ASIC project our seed money. It was our customers who showed us how to become a great ASIC supplier. But most importantly for me personally, it was the customer that gave me power and air cover among management. No one would dare to argue or decline when I called them to a meeting with a well-known customer. It didn't matter which division they were in or where they were in the management chain. Our customers gave me the power to interact with anyone in management, all the way up to the IBM boardroom. It didn't matter that I was just a lowly manager. I was interacting with people who were our customers *and* competitors, and that gave me the power to get things done without a lot of questions being asked.

That power didn't come without challenges, though, especially from those above me who were upset that some upstart second-line manager was working directly with IBM's CEO (seven levels above me!) and the Division General Manager (six levels above me). Basically, I was a thorn in the side of everyone who was one to five levels above me!

My direct manager, Ken, was definitely feeling a little frustrated with me. He was very smart, but also opinionated and fairly rigid about opposing points of view. He and I would hold regular one-on-one meetings, and while much of our conversations focused on business and the tasks at hand, he also liked to talk about his personal life and career. I got the impression that Ken felt that part of my role was to listen and give him support with his personal issues.

One day, I came into our meeting with some new ideas on how we could propel our business forward. These weren't Ken's ideas, so he disagreed with every single one of them and summarily dismissed me. He said, "Chris, you make a great lieutenant, but you'll never be a general."[1] That stung a bit, but it was nothing compared to discovering in my next review that Ken thought my performance was slipping (I had always been a top performer and received the highest appraisal ratings). I felt the assessment was unfair, but rather than "sweat the small stuff," I decided to try an experiment. I would listen to Ken's stories and complaints about the home front and resist challenging his ideas or bringing new ones of my own. Disappointingly, but unsurprisingly, Ken's assessment of my performance did a 180. He thought I was doing great, and my ratings went back up! Later, after I had been promoted to running IBM's Microelectronics division, I had a chance to see the history of IBM's development plan for me as an "up and coming" female manager. I was equal parts surprised and amused by how low my managers' aspirations for me had been over the years (one manager said I "might be able to rise to a second-line manager"). I guess Ken wasn't the only one who didn't see me as "general material."

Ultimately, Ken's and others' opinions of me didn't really matter, though. My customer and business success meant that he couldn't stand in my way. When faced with situations like the one I faced with Ken, we have a choice to make. Do we focus on that individual battle or the overall war? I always focus on what really matters. In this case, the customer success we were creating would translate into financial success, and that's what mattered to senior management.

There were challenges, though, as we moved from the early startup phase to our adolescence. Our growing customer base loved our ASICs—from our silicon technology, to our design methodology, to our packaging—and our operations, but they were concerned about working with the behemoth IBM. They were worried about supply reliability; that we would prioritize IBM's own ASIC needs during times of high demand and they would be neglected. I assuaged their concerns by committing myself and my team to their success, but at this point we were still largely a startup so that commitment meant my team and I were running our engine in the RPM red zone every day. My days were filled with sales calls and pitches, drafting pricing and financial deals, legal contract work, and managing the design and development teams. I set tough goals for both my team and myself, but the team consistently rose to meet my challenges and were almost flawless in their execution.

The outside world began to take notice of our success, and some were quite vocal in their opposition. Our competitor ASIC suppliers, like LSI Logic and VLSI, naturally pooh-poohed our efforts as unnecessary given the maturity of the market. Even the industry trade publications took aim at us, asking, "Who needs *another* ASIC supplier?" Design-tool providers also fired their shots at us, including the CEO of Synopsys, Art Degeus.[2]

None of those naysayers could argue with our success, though. The revenue we were generating had allowed our team to grow to almost 300 people and had resulted in my being promoted to third-line management again, overseeing the entire ASIC organization. By 1997, our group had grown to $1 billion in annual revenue, and the industry analyst firm Dataquest stated that we had become the number-one ASIC provider in North America (much to LSI Logic's and VLSI's chagrin). We had made it!

Lesson #9—The Power of the Customer

Companies have numerous stakeholders—employees, customers, investors, partners, industry associations, governments, communities, and so on. Each of these stakeholders can have numerous subgroups, and each of these subgroups has its own visions, goals, and priorities. Navigating the web of agenda in the average company requires a balance and deftness that only comes with years of experience (and sometimes not even then). I learned early on, though, that if you focus on the stakeholders that carry the greatest weight and align your agenda with their agenda, their center of gravity tends to bring the other stakeholders along.

As the source of revenue and profitability, customers are almost always the most critical stakeholder in a company. If you align your work to their priorities, everything else tends to align as well. That's not to say that "the customer is always right." The customer may not always know what they most need and want, especially if you haven't created and shown them a better path yet. Prior to Apple creating a touchscreen keyboard on the iPhone, everyone thought they wanted a physical keyboard on their smartphones. By keeping its customers' priorities for form *and* function in mind, however, Apple launched a stylish iPhone whose pop-up touchscreen keyboard enabled a larger screen for new smartphone applications like video. Our customers wanted us to align with the LSI and VLSI chip-design processes, until we showed them a faster way to get their chips to market. It's not the customers' stated wants or needs that matter most—it's what will make them most successful.

If you understand how to make your customers successful, and align your work to serving that end, you will find the rest of your company tends to fall in line behind you as customers reward you with the revenue and profitability that are the lifeblood of any organization. I began to truly understand that with my first big customer, Unisys. When Unisys called me into that senior executive meeting in Bluebell, Pennsylvania, and made it clear to IBM's executives that they were relying on me and my team to help them successfully bring their chips to market, they opened an important door for me. Suddenly, the work I was doing gained strategic importance, executive visibility, and most importantly, executive support. The power of the customer is that it opens doors and smooths your path.

That's not to say your life will always be easy. Throughout my career, I faced skepticism about my abilities and suspicion of my non-IBM way of doing things from managers, peers, and even direct reports. They put obstacles in my way because I operated outside the norm (or maybe it was just plain sexism), but those obstacles could always be swept away by the power of the customer. Whenever I had a customer meeting, engineers from every group would want an invitation. They may not have liked the way I was doing things, but they couldn't argue with my customer results. This let me leapfrog over all the normal constraints of doing business, and I didn't have to hit them over the head with those results to get things done. I could just say, "Well, customer X is going to want us to do it this way," and people knew they needed to get on board. Customers are your ace in the hole.

Lou Gerstner's tour of our division in Burlington, Vermont, only reinforced this perspective. IBM prided itself on its technology, and rightly so, but what most interested Lou when he visited were my customers. After quickly moving through all the other groups' technology demonstrations, Lou ended up spending more time at our demo than any other because it allowed him to speak with our customers and see the impact we were having on their success. It was particularly gratifying to watch Qualcomm wow Lou with their new phone after being criticized earlier for wasting my time on them. At the end of that visit, IBM's CEO told our site manager to "take care of me" because the customers liked me.

In your own career, it's critical to examine your situation to understand who is paying the bills, who is the source of your organization's revenue and profitability, and align the work you are doing to their success. Beyond those external customers, you also have "customers" in your organization. What will make them successful? What are their priorities? Understand your customers' priorities, help them achieve success, and everything else will fall into place.

Notes

1   Despite his prediction, in less than a decade I would be his boss's boss's boss.

2   Ironically, Deirdre Hanford, Director of Strategic Relationships at Synopsys, and Chi-Foon Chan, their president, would later broker a deal with me (in 1996) to buy and license our tools so that they could sell them to the rest of the industry, which would propel us to overall market leadership. In their rush to close the deal, they interrupted my vacation and visited me when I was at The Big E, an agricultural fair in Massachusetts, with my dairy cows!

Chapter 9

Flying Through Turbulence (1997–1999)

By 1997 we had grown so successful that IBM leadership decided that our group should become its own product line with its own general manager (GM). I was excited! I had built the ASIC business from the ground up. I was its mother. This was my chance to finally become an IBM executive!

The powers that be were busy planning the creation of the new ASIC product line, so I kept going about my business. One day, as I was preparing for a meeting with Cray, I asked Jim Picciano's administrative assistant for an organizational chart that I could share with the customer. She handed me an org chart that had me in the GM role! I was so excited, but since the division and its leadership hadn't been announced yet, I kept it to myself (and didn't show it to Cray).

Days passed, and then a couple of weeks, and nothing happened. My excitement began to dim and transform into concern about the announcement delay. When the announcement of the new division was finally released, I was dumbfounded to discover that I was not named the GM. Bruce Beers, one of the "good ol' boys" in the IBM hierarchy, had been tapped as the new GM instead of me. Bruce was a great general manager, but he didn't know *anything* about our business and I'm sure he was as surprised as I was by being given this assignment. I had grown it from nothing to more than $1 billion in a couple of years, and I lost the leadership of my organization because of the good ol' boy network. I was, in a word, angry. In another word, I was crushed.

So, I went through the motions at work and cried at home over the next few days. I felt cheated and utterly mistreated by IBM. But once again, I pulled myself together and began looking for a path forward. I was guided by two principles—"Do the right thing" and "If you can't go through, go around." That is, if I couldn't get to the executive level following the path I had been on, I would find a new path.

I "did the right thing" by committing to spending six months getting Bruce up to speed on the ASIC business. I had built the business and knew everything about it from every angle. I owed it to the business and my team to transfer as much of that knowledge as possible to Bruce. I spent hours in his office writing on his whiteboard and explaining the technical concepts behind our business. I took him on the road to introduce him to our customers. I spent hours with him going over every customer's personality and reviewing their contracts. It took every minute of those six months, but when I was done, Bruce was ready to fly on his own.

Now, it was time to find my own new path. Around that time, I was sitting in a meeting with several high-level IBM executives, including the head of sales for IBM Microelectronics, John Gleason. John was an unusual IBM executive because he'd been hired from Hitachi and wasn't an IBM insider. We knew each other since we had done some work together, and he was the executive who had been assigned to keep me and my customers "in line" during Lou Gerstner's earlier visit. I liked John and knew that he was like me; someone who focused on the corporate mission more than corporate politics. John was someone who was open to new ideas and new people (including people outside IBM) as long as they contributed to building a world-class organization and helped him get the job done.

During that meeting, I was struck by an awareness and idea with the same life-altering forcefulness as my experience at that gas station so many years before. I realized that staying within my current management chain would only lead to additional disappointment and heartache. I recognized that if building a $1 billion business didn't earn me a leadership role in that group, nothing would. Bob Dylan's plaintive lyric, "There must be some way out of here," came rushing back into my head, but this time I knew the way out. I needed to go around that group to get to where I wanted to be, and I realized with crystal clarity that John and the Sales organization was the path I needed to take.

At the time, IBM Microelectronics didn't have a significant field applications engineering organization to help customers design products with IBM chips and solutions. Spotting that gap, I walked up to John at the water fountain during a break in the meeting and said, "I have a proposition for you. If you hire me and promote me to an executive within Sales, I will build you the best field applications engineering unit on the planet."

John looked at me for a second and then responded, "That sounds pretty good. Let me see what I can do."

Within a week, John created and offered me a Director of Field Applications Engineering position within the IBM Microelectronics Products division; my first executive position! That same day, Jim Picciano, the executive whose team had given Bruce the GM position of the ASIC business instead of me, called me into his office. He said, "I hear you have an offer to work in Sales and we will approve it. You will no doubt be good at it, you'll have a lot of fun, and you will make a lot of money. *But* you will never be able to come back to engineering development!"

I joked to myself, *Okay, so what's the downside?*

Seriously, though, the idea that I would have fun and make lots of money at something that I would be good at sounded just about perfect to me.

Finally, I was an executive—IBM Microelectronics' first female executive! It was a global role supporting all of IBM's semiconductor products, including memory, PowerPC microprocessors, and of course the ASIC business that was growing like gangbusters. Once again, I was starting from scratch with only a handful of people, fewer than ten, to span the globe. One of my first priorities was to find an enthusiastic leader for each of our geographies: North America, Europe, and Asia. I kept Michael Massetti as my US leader and hired David Cremese from France to run Europe. One of IBM's technology experts, Tien Wu, had heard about what I was doing, was attracted to the potential of the new venture, and requested the leadership position in Asia. Tien had spent his entire career worrying about microns and molecules, but my team represented an opportunity for him to learn about customers and business. He was so enthusiastic when we spoke that I took a chance on him. It turned out to be a great call, as Tien has risen to magnificent heights in his career and is now the CEO of Advanced Semiconductor Engineering (ASE), one of the largest companies in Taiwan.

My first task was to meet with my team and customers, which meant an around-the-world trip. I had never been to Asia before and started the first of my many Asian journeys in Japan, before flying on to Singapore and finally Taiwan, where our extremely talented engineers lived and breathed technology. Over time, I would come to foster many great relationships in Asia, and Taiwan became like a second home to me thanks to its technology-savvy culture.

I struggled a little more in Japan as a woman, at least at first. In the 1990s, the only women I saw in Japanese companies were the stylishly dressed assistants who invariably came into every meeting serving coffee. IBM was targeting the gaming industry in Japan as a potentially lucrative market for our technology. We had our biggest win when Nintendo selected the PowerPC for their systems. We wanted to replicate that success at smaller companies like Sega. So, I set out to win that business as well, feeling my collaborative style would enable us to win the account. I was excited over the course of our meetings that I seemed to make great headway with the Sega team and they agreed to most of the terms of the deal. I toasted myself on our success on the flight home, only to get a phone call the next day from the senior engineer from the Sega team. "King-san, we are very sorry, but we cannot agree to the terms we discussed when you were in Japan."

To my dismay, they hadn't really meant anything they had said (they were afraid to say no to me in person) and I discovered I was right back at square one. I discovered through that experience that I had a reputation in Japan—"King-san is very fair, but very tough!"

That said, my experience was quite the opposite when I presented IBM's new planar semiconductor technology at an industry forum in Tokyo. Our new technology was an industry breakthrough that allowed much greater connectivity with copper wiring. This was *big* news in Japan because it enabled a huge jump in circuit density, allowing them to pack more computing power into a smaller package. I was presenting the technology in a large hall with a translator. When I walked on to the brightly lit stage, I was astounded to be greeted by an audience of more than a thousand Japanese men. The speech went well. Everyone was hanging on to every word of my technically complex presentation. After the session was over, there was a reception and a line of Japanese executives, each with his own interpreter, waiting to ask me questions. I was surprised to learn that these were the top executives of every Japanese technology company, including Hitachi, Toshiba, Fujitsu, and NEC. Everyone was very respectful and somewhat in awe of me and our technology. I learned that when it comes to technology knowledge, gender boundaries dissolve, even in Japan.

Working for John Gleason put me in an unusual and often powerful position. IBM Microelectronics had never had a sales group before since their only customer was IBM. So, when John came along and was selling chips outside IBM, there was nobody inside IBM to take key positions, and John had to hire externally to find sales executives to run the three geographies, sales engineers, inside salespeople, and so on. These individuals were all quite smart and certainly knew their stuff, but they didn't know "the IBM way." As a result, I became the bridge and "corporate translator" between the sales executives and IBM, Inc., making a number of wonderful, lasting relationships along the way.

It was also new for me to be working with these non-IBMers. When John held his executive meetings, the environment was more freewheeling and fun than the typical stodgy IBM meeting. I really began to enjoy the camaraderie and competitiveness of this unusual group, but I learned to be careful with how far I went with trying to fit in with the boys. Once, after a meeting, everyone lit up a cigar in one hand while holding an after-dinner cocktail in the other. I was the only female present, of course, and while I wasn't a smoker, I figured this was the price of entry to being "one of the boys." When I woke up the next morning, however, the cigar smoke and drinking from the night before had left me queasy and I decided I didn't need to be one of the boys *that* badly.

At first, I wasn't able to build my team very quickly or significantly, and as our business grew around the world, we began to run into scaling challenges. For example, 3Com, the developer of the first modems, asked me to visit their engineering facility in Tel Aviv.[1] I met with the head of their operation, and I was elated when he said that we had won their business, but he also said that the business came with a caveat—we would have to put two engineers on site for the two years it would take to complete the design. As it would turn out, finding two engineers willing to relocate to Tel Aviv was one of the biggest challenges I would face. But I wouldn't give up and I finally found a Jewish engineer in another division who wanted to give his family an Israeli experience and a hippie who enjoyed traveling the world. While I had somehow managed to provide the local support 3Com needed, it was clear I needed a more sustainable local support model in the future.

IBM Microelectronics wasn't doing so well, though, and budgets were tight. So, I racked my brain for a solution to how we could meet the demand for our field engineering services with a small staff and shoestring budget. And then I had a novel idea. What if instead of sending our field engineers to individual customers all over the world, a process that isn't very scalable with a small team, we created a central location in Vermont and regional field design centers where customers could come for help in creating and executing their designs? The design centers would be located relatively close to our customers, and in some cases our engineers could actually work at the customer facilities as part of their team. It was a concept that I would quickly discover customers loved and would pay for. I also discovered how valuable it was to me and IBM as the centers were great at keeping competitors out, away from our customers, and they gave us unique insights into our customers' future plans.

I had maintained contact with my old team and customers in the ASIC business, so those customers were some of my first field design center customers, and I was able to recruit one of my old development managers, Mike O'Neill, to manage the centers. I renamed my group "Field Engineering," and the demand and revenue we were generating allowed my group to quickly grow to 300 people. I am a strong believer in close communications, and with an engineering group spread across the globe, I knew that the best way to bring together different cultures and countries was through our common language and love of technology. So, I started holding an annual Field Engineering meeting, as well as smaller regional meetings, to bring engineers from around the world together to share ideas about how we could better support our customers.

Our first meeting was in Boston, which was an exciting trip for many of our engineers who had never had the opportunity to travel to the United States. In the technical sessions, we concentrated on ideas and ways we could bring even better technology to our customers. I always found competition was a great way to get everyone thinking and creating in these meetings. We held competitions, from contests to discover who had the best technical ideas, to *Jeopardy*-like quizzes to see which team knew the most. I arranged the questions so that the playing field was level and an engineer from Taiwan would have the same chance of winning as someone from Chicago. There was always a lot of cheering and energy during these competitions.

One night, I rented a boat in Boston Harbor and we had lobster for dinner. Lobster was a treat for some of our team members, and I remember being shocked as I watched some of them eat as many as seven lobsters in one sitting (and they weren't small!). We went to a Red Sox baseball game to give the group an experience of American culture. I was struck by the cultural differences and laughed when David Cremese, our European leader from France, saw a runner steal a base and asked me, "Is he authorized to do that?"

When the game was over one of the Taiwanese engineers commented to me, "You think this is a baseball game? You should see a game in Taipei!" Of course, on my next trip to Taiwan I did just that. He was right. US fans are nothing compared to the Taiwanese. The spectators had every type of noisemaker possible and were on their feet cheering loudly until the last minute of the game, even though our team was eight runs behind. It was amazing!

As my group continued to grow, the center of power for the ASIC business shifted from my old internal team that Bruce now ran to my new field team. Now that we were providing engineering support at customers' facilities, the internal team became merely the back-office group maintaining the technology. I was the customer-facing executive, driving our chips into all of Cisco's, Ericsson's, Cray's, and other companies' products, and though the internal team got credit for the revenue we were bringing in, if Mike Attardo had a question he came to me, not to Bruce. All the energy was in the field, and we were the ones who drove the ASIC business to more than $2 billion in revenue and number-one market leadership in the world just over five years after we launched, which was both humbling and personally satisfying to me.

As our group and business took off, John backed me all the way. It was actually quite refreshing to have a boss who authentically supported me and wanted me to succeed. He included me in his planning and strategy meetings. He trusted and relied on me to cover all the technical bases. I remember one time when John and I were talking before a meeting in the San Francisco Bay area and he blurted out, "Chris, you have it all! There doesn't appear to be anything you can't do, and I know that you're going to have a great career." That was the first time I had ever heard something so genuinely positive from my manager. I was surprised and incredibly grateful for his comments and support. In 1998, John added responsibility for IBM Microelectronics' Marketing to my role and promoted me to vice president, which was another first for me *and* IBM Microelectronics (first female vice president)!

My star was rising and Dr. John Kelly III, who had a PhD in materials science and led research at IBM, and my GM Mike Attardo (also a PhD) invited me to dinner. Their invitation baffled me a bit, but I enjoyed the dinner and the great Ferrari Carano wine they ordered. What I most enjoyed, however, was the conversation and being told once again that I would have a great career at IBM (and coincidentally, how good I would look in a Porsche!). I had been tagged as "high potential," and was being groomed for bigger things. It was hard to take in the fact that I was sitting at dinner with two of the top executives in IBM, and they were toasting me!

Meanwhile, Lou Gerstner was shaking things up. He appointed Jim Vanderslice, who had previously run IBM's storage division, to be the new Technology group GM in early 1998. When Mike Attardo retired in early 1999, Lou promoted John Kelly to be the new Microelectronics division GM. When those appointments were announced, I realized why it had been Mike and John Kelly who had taken me out to dinner—it was the outgoing general manager along with the incoming one. These were good appointments, but changes at the top often cascade down throughout the organization, and not always in ways that benefit everyone lower down in the hierarchy.

I heard rumors that Jim would be centralizing sales under the Technology group and bringing in his own sales leader. That didn't bode well for my boss, John Gleason (or me), since John would most likely choose to leave rather than be part of the new organizational and reporting structure. John Gleason was my biggest fan, and if he ended up leaving, I wondered and worried about what it would mean for me.

Within the Microelectronics division, as soon as John Kelly was named the head of the division, he asked for a meeting with me. He wanted to know all about our ASIC business, but he was especially interested in our customers. He asked about our relationships with them and what their goals and objectives were. I enjoyed speaking with him and had fun talking with a seasoned technology expert.

One of the first things John Kelly did was to reorganize the division by end-market segments—computing, wired communications, wireless communications, storage, and pervasive or distributed computing—each of which would have its own leader. These business units would become centers of power within the Microelectronics group; both the customer interface and the authority on resource investments, product development, and revenue and profitability. It sounded as if sales and my field engineering group might be deprioritized in the new organizational structure. Again, this could be bad for me, and my anxiety continued to grow. I wondered if I would still have a job after all of these restructurings or would again find myself on the losing end when the dust settled.

Finally, after weeks of fretting over conference calls and trying to read the tea leaves of where the organization was headed, I received another call from John Kelly. He confirmed that there would be five divisions in Microelectronics based on end markets. "One of the divisions will be new, Chris—Wired Communications—and I think you're the best person to run it as General Manager."

Wow, I thought to myself, excited by the opportunity but mostly just relieved after all the anxiety and worry!

Thinking back on that conversation, I give John a lot of credit for taking a chance on me. I wasn't the typical executive choice (I was definitely *not* part of IBM's good ol' boy network), but John wasn't a typical IBM leader, and he was willing to place his bet on my experience in creating and rapidly growing the ASIC and field engineering businesses and on my strong relationships with IBM's network equipment manufacturing customers.

"I had been out with [Chris] to key customers, and the bottom line was that they had huge trust in her," he later said.[2] He told me that my "what you see is what you get" authenticity made *everyone* trust me—customers, employees, management—and that authenticity coupled with my intelligence and resilience made me a good bet. His bet on me would end up being a *very* good bet.[3]

Lesson #10—When You Can't Go Through, Go Around

It is said that the definition of insanity is doing the same thing over and over again, hoping for a different result. I have a strong work ethic and hate to fail at something I am working on, but there are times in your life when success or failure is outside your control. There are times when simply working harder or smarter on the path you are on will simply not yield the results you want. In those cases, it is insane to just keep following the same path, hoping it will lead to a more positive result.

When the ASICs business that I had built from the ground up was taken away from me and given to someone else, it was the second big gut-punch of my career. I realized through that experience that there are situations where your success is completely outside your control. My goal was to become an executive, and if building a billion-dollar business from scratch wasn't sufficient in my current management structure to get there, it was time to pursue a different path. I have learned that the path to success is rarely linear and straightforward.

But how do you know your path is truly blocked and not merely difficult? Everyone has hard times at work, sometimes exceedingly hard times. You can have difficult managers, difficult customers, difficult projects. The young engineer I was working with in my first year as a manager might have viewed me as a difficult boss forcing him to work on a difficult project.[4] In the end, though, he accomplished the project and thanked me for the role I had played in spurring him on and supporting him to finish the project. What a shame it would have been if he had thought he was being blocked and had given up on the project and himself prematurely!

So, how do you determine whether your path is blocked versus merely difficult? I answer that question with three different questions. First, is there a runway for success? That is, do you have enough space and time to achieve your goals within the current path? For example, if there is space to take on more responsibility and be promoted beyond the immediate difficulties, it might be worthwhile sticking it out. If, however, the time it will take you to achieve those goals exceeds the time you have, due to, for example, retirement or some other competing goal, maybe it is time to move on.

The second question to ask is, is your path destined for failure? That is, when you objectively look at your environment, the assets and resources that are available to you, and the mandate with which you have been charged, are you going to fail no matter what you put into it? This is a difficult situation to assess for yourself and it is best to have a mentor or friend to help you. Toward the end of my career at IBM, I realized that despite all the power I had, I didn't control a key element that would determine my ultimate success or failure, and that element was pointing toward my ultimate failure. At that point, I knew it was time to move on.

The final question to ask is, are you still learning new and useful things? If so, there may be value in sticking it out. If your knowledge acquisition is stagnating, however, it's time to go.

"Going around" can mean different things. You can go around within your organization, as I did when I pivoted from development and managing the ASIC business to sales and managing ASIC field engineering. That usually requires an organization that is large enough to accommodate multiple paths to success. The other option of going around is leaving the organization to start somewhere new that offers a path to success. One of the women I coach, who is in the insurance industry, recently realized that she had explored and exhausted all the potential pathways she had in her current company. It was time for her to "go around" the blockage by moving on to a new company.

Regardless of whether you "go around" within or outside your organization, it takes courage, but we're talking about your life and your goals. Don't let fear stand in the way of pursuing your vision, even if it means striking out in unknown new directions. As they say, you rarely regret the shots you take. It's the shots you don't take that will haunt you.

Notes

1   When I walked down the jetway at Ben Gurion International airport I felt like I was stepping back in history. Israel is one of the most diverse countries in the world, but the machine guns everywhere took some getting used to.

2   Wood, Robert Chapman and Michael L. Tushman, "IBM Network Technology (A)," Harvard Business School Publishing, 2001.

3   Being named the GM of the Wired Communications division also felt like a rebirth of my career at IBM. I loved working for John Gleason, but he was always viewed as somewhat of an IBM outsider, so having my wagon hitched to his branded me as an outsider as well (and my renegade reputation didn't help with that). With John Kelly tapping me as GM, I was being brought back into the "inner circle."

4   This story is recounted in Chapter 4.

Chapter 10

Scanning the Horizon (1999–2001)

John Kelly was the second manager who took a real interest in my career and authentically wanted me to succeed. After he appointed me General Manager of the Wired Communications group, I started spending more time with him. He was very smart, with a PhD in materials science from Rensselaer Polytechnic Institute. He looked and acted like a real executive, with a regal bearing (but inquisitive and eager to learn), and was consistently cool, calm, and collected. We made an odd couple—him, the gentleman executive, and me, the street fighter—but it worked!

We spent much of those first weeks together talking about customers. After running the ASIC group and Microelectronics field engineering group, I understood our customers, their challenges, and how they thought better than just about anyone else at IBM. Since John was still relatively new to his position, he came to me for insights into our customers, our products, and how to bring them together. Once again, I gave my manager an executive training "crash course" in customers and our business, and John soaked it up like a sponge. It wasn't to be a one-direction flow of information and ideas, however. As I said, John was brilliant, and I would learn much from him over the months and years to come.

As General Manager of Wired Communications, I had responsibility for the full financial performance, or P&L (profit and loss), of the group and for many of the ASIC customers I had originally brought to IBM and who were now going into full production: Cisco, Juniper, Ericsson, Alcatel, and numerous smaller and startup companies. Manufacturing, sales, and development engineering remained separate groups, but

I would be funding them, and as they say, "money talks." For the first time in my career, I felt I could dictate the direction and pace of my organization and largely control all the necessary levers for success.

But in what was starting to feel like a recurring bad dream, my nascent Wired Communications group didn't come with any staff. For the third time in my career, I was left to fend for myself while the other GMs were given full, existing organizations. When I asked John about this, he said that unlike my peers, I had proven myself with building strong teams and that it would be better if I were allowed to create a team from scratch.

While he may have been buttering me up, he was right, and I enjoyed the benefit of being able to design my organization for maximum effectiveness without any of the baggage of a pre-existing structure. I was able to cherry-pick my team from people I knew and who had proven themselves. Plus, by that point I had developed a reputation as an "IBM entrepreneur" (an oxymoron if ever there was one) who created billion-dollar businesses from nothing. That created a center of gravity within IBM that drew amazing, creative people to me.

It was clear at that point that John Gleason would be leaving IBM, so his organization began to collapse. There were good people in his organization who, like John, were less than enthusiastic about the new sales structure. As a result, I was able to recruit three people from the marketing organization I had previously run, including the head of operations Victor Lee, Steve Longoria (who would eventually go on to become the CEO of MicroTech), and a promising new college graduate, Ben Schlatka (who went on to eventually co-found and lead his own company, MC10). I also added Rob Gibson, who had been managing customer support for my old ASIC group, and Duncan Needler, who came from the PowerPC group to help me manage product marketing and ensure our customers understood all that we could do for them. And, of course, Ann Rincon joined my team again.

Then, I lucked out again by having another division shut down that provided me access to the great engineers I would need. IBM's networking business in Raleigh, North Carolina, had been focused on applications based on the token ring networking protocol, but then the Ethernet protocol won the market. Jim Vanderslice said I could hire as many of those engineers as I wanted, and that engineering group brought critical networking expertise and experience to our group, as well as an interesting product portfolio.

With our resources starting to line up, my leadership team and I started speaking to the networking industry's leaders, many of whom already used our ASICs, from the long-haul guys like Alcatel and Ericsson, to the networking experts like Cisco and Juniper, to the startups that would disrupt the industry with their new ideas and technologies. Everyone was working to build out the internet as quickly as possible, and we worked with them to determine their biggest needs and to find the gaps that we could fill. We reviewed IBM's existing and emerging products and strengths in manufacturing to find the best matches. We knew we had a strong starting position with our current customers and existing ASIC business, but we also knew bigger things were possible. We were developing a set of powerful new products—from long-distance optical lines to intelligent processors—that would dramatically increase the reliability and performance of the internet. These technologies would allow us to extend our business into exciting new growth and emerging opportunities at the dawn of the internet era.

Then, we started thinking about the financial results we would commit to. We threw ourselves into developing business cases, spending untold hours on determining what was possible. David Balkin, who would eventually work for me, said:

People who had little business experience [in other words, my fledgling team] were cranking on business cases till the cows came home. They were able to turn a spreadsheet faster than I could write my name. They were relentless go-getters who were going to figure out how to win.[1]

And we were. From the very beginning, our aspirations were big. When we looked at the market we were targeting, whose leader, Lucent, commanded only 11% market share, we knew we could be a billion-dollar business in just a couple of years. Our plan was to increase our sales by five times in 2000 on the way to becoming the number-one chip supplier to network equipment manufacturers by 2003. Research firm International Business Strategies (IBS) pointed out that we would need to grow to more than $3 billion over the next few years to accomplish that feat. Anyone outside our group would have thought we were crazy to think like that. In fact, more than one IBM executive asked us, "What are you smoking?" when they saw our business plans calling for year-over-year triple-digit growth.

Our ambition was unusual for IBM, and my penchant for setting big goals and somehow achieving them became an asset for John Kelly and a source of annoyance for my peers. John had a monthly operations and status meeting, during which he would have the GMs report on their organization's status and financial results. We all had revenue targets to hit (my target for the first year was $300 million), and at one of these meetings, several of my peers were having trouble hitting their targets. It quickly became clear that these shortfalls meant that our division was going to miss its overall revenue targets. John turned to me (the only one who was creating an organization from scratch, mind you), and asked, "Chris, can you commit to $20 million more?" I, of course, said, "Yes." The other GMs blanched, either in embarrassment or disbelief. Tom Reeves, who ran the storage business, protested, "She can't make those numbers!" But we did.

We always did. I credit my success to always approaching customers and contracts from a win-win perspective to craft a deal that was fair and reasonable for all parties. While that may seem like a no-brainer approach, it was not "the IBM way." IBM viewed itself as the 800-pound gorilla in the industry and believed that all customers should accept its terms and be grateful for the opportunity to work with IBM. That may have been okay before we started working with equally formidable customers like Cisco, Ericsson, and HP, but when dealing with other 800-pound gorillas, we needed to behave differently. That approach came naturally to me, but IBM struggled to adapt. So, getting these contracts through the legal department was always a hassle for me. No one seemed to recognize that we needed to approach contracts with an eye toward securing a win for both sides in order to get these customers to commit millions of dollars of business to us.

I remember being at my wits' end looking at a contract in my office late one night. HP was visiting us the next day to complete the contract for the first million-gate design and I knew that they would be appalled at the IBM contract I currently had in my hands. It was so one-sided and I hadn't been able to get the attorney I was working with to budge on the contract's content.

I turned to IBM's online directory, where you could trace anyone's management chain. I looked up the attorney I was working with and saw that his boss was someone named Darlene Gerry who had an office in New York. Even though it was late I tried her number and she answered. I discovered that she had recently been appointed to run the legal team for IBM Microelectronics. I explained my situation to her and what the customer expected. She saw my point immediately, saying that she wouldn't sign the current contract if she were the customer. I asked her what I should do. I was running out of time. The customer was arriving in less than 12 hours at 8:00 a.m. She floored me when she said that she would rewrite the contract overnight and I would have it in my hands before the customer showed up. *Finally!* I thought. *Someone gets it!*

From then on, whenever I needed to put together a contract, Darlene would be my "go to" attorney, and she always stepped right up. Whether I was at Ericsson in Stockholm or Cisco in California, Darlene would come with me for difficult negotiations or be on the phone with us. Eventually, the big bosses realized how far we had strayed from the accepted IBM way and forbade us to do any more business together. I had to start working with other attorneys who would presumably provide a better check and balance to me and my contracts. That said, whenever I had a tough legal question, I would grab Darlene and we would meet in a closet somewhere (literally!) so we wouldn't be seen by the powers that be. Darlene ultimately left IBM to become the assistant District Attorney for Portland, Maine (I think it was her own version of "If you can't go through, go around"), but I enticed her to rejoin the private sector when I became CEO at AMI Semiconductor, and she became my General Counsel for the next seven years.

My ability to buck the system and get customers signed was how I earned the nickname "Let's-Make-A-Deal Chris." In talking to my customers, IBS CEO Handel Jones, one of the leading semiconductor industry analysts and consultants, remarked:

I deal directly with a lot of customers of IBM [and] a lot of them have told me: "The one thing that is unique about Chris King is that Chris King listens to us. Which means that she will find out what we really need and go back and explain to the engineers that they have to make it for us." She will fight for the customer in the company.[2]

I always put the customer first, committing to meeting their needs, even if we didn't yet have the capabilities, as long as I believed we would be able to. John Kelly said:

> Half of my organization saw Chris as out-of-control, making commitments that were going to be difficult to keep, working with customers that were not like our traditional ones...A lot of people didn't understand that...I remember going from one site to the next in the organization, saying, "It's either grow or die. We have done the strategy analysis, and Chris is the person to execute it."[3]

Not that it was easy. In a hypergrowth environment like that, you never have enough capacity or resources and must be creative to meet the demand. So, once again, I played the role of conductor in the orchestra, aligning IBM's broader sales, development, and manufacturing functions (and even outside manufacturers) to set and meet audacious goals. I was a bulldog when it came to meeting our customers' needs, working tirelessly to win over the naysayers. My executive assistant David Higgins quipped, "Chris is a terrific salesperson. If you can say no to her, you're better than we are. If you think she's gone away, you'll see her coming in the window."[4] I had to convince our design teams to adapt their processes to achieve both superior performance *and* rapid time to market. At first, the engineers chafed at my requests, but eventually the excitement of our business won them over! I had to convince manufacturing to invest in capabilities and capacity for products that weren't clearly defined. I had to convince other members of IBM's senior management that we could actually do what we were setting out to do. At one management meeting, someone had questioned the always conservative Tom Reeves about his uninspiring business goals and performance, to which he quipped, "At least we didn't set unrealistic objectives like *some* people." Sitting in that meeting, I knew who the "some people" he was referring to were.

The fact was that I ran my business completely differently from my peers. From their perspective, I was undisciplined and not doing things "the IBM way."[5] Having built my business from the ground up my way, however, I was intimately familiar with every aspect of its operation and could execute with an agility and mastery that others simply couldn't. This was apparent when Jim Vanderslice would come to review the Microelectronics business periodically. The five business units would present to him in these meetings, and like Lou Gerstner, Jim didn't want you to walk him through a boring slide deck. He wanted you to be fluent in your business and able to stand up in the front of the room without notes to talk about your strategy and the details of your customers, competitors, products, financial results, and outlook. That was my wheelhouse and I always shone.

By the fall, our business was growing extremely rapidly, and John Kelly decided that Lou Gerstner needed to hear more about what we were doing. We were invited to present to Lou and his senior staff in Armonk, which was a big deal. So, John and I drove to Armonk, and as we were riding the elevator up to the executive conference room in which we would be meeting, John leaned over and whispered to me, "Lou has a short attention span. He has a lot on his mind, so don't be surprised if he starts looking at his email and doesn't pay attention to you."

We'll see about that, I thought to myself.

Once we were in the room with all of Lou's executive staff, including the CFO, General Counsel, and Sam Palmisano (who would become the next CEO of IBM in 2002), I could see that Lou ruled the roost and that everyone deferred to him. Even John Kelly was a bit nervous. After John introduced me and my business, I started my presentation, and as predicted, Lou's attention drifted to his computer. In my head I was thinking,

Lou is GOING to pay attention to me, and having presented to him back in my ASIC days, I knew what would get his attention—money and customers. So, I veered off script and blurted out that "Our business is on track to achieve $1 billion of revenue over the next year with the largest customers in the networking industry, including Cisco, Juniper, and Ericsson."

Lou's head popped up and I had his eyes and attention for the rest of the meeting as I described how we would become indispensable to our customers and achieve exceptional levels of success. John was amazed at how well the presentation went. As we got back into the elevator, he turned to me and said, "Chris, you just hit the ball out of the park!" Just by knowing my business inside and out and having a dogged determination to succeed, I had been able to win over Lou Gerstner, who became an enthusiastic fan of mine. As I left the elevator with John, I was walking on air.

Having Lou Gerstner as a supporter (and John Kelly as my boss) cleared out just about any obstacle I ran into. I received the resources and support I needed, which allowed us to continue growing like gangbusters. Suddenly, our business was in the limelight.

John regularly communicated with his many teams across the division as he visited the various sites. Everyone wanted to see the new Division GM, and his sessions were regularly packed with 100–200 people squeezed into auditoriums and large conference rooms. John asked me to come along with him and present my business in these sessions. He always introduced Wired Communications as the fastest-growing group in the division and talked about how important our customers were and how critical we were to the overall division's success. He touted my leadership of the group, which really gave me confidence. The audiences often included many of my former colleagues and even my old bosses. When I got up to deliver my presentations, I lit up the room with my passion, humorous stories about our team's scrappy startup culture (as well as our phenomenal accomplishments), and customer stories. John was clearly proud of what I was doing and how I came across in these large meetings. And it was fun for me!

Lou also talked about us, and once when I had my team gathered at IBM's headquarters for a strategy meeting, Lou showed up to meet the team and listen in to our strategic brainstorming. The team liked that attention from the CEO, and other groups recognized that we were doing something interesting enough to bring Lou to the table. That was something.

It was also around this time that my own financial success really started to take off. Lou called me into his office during that period and awarded me a special $1 million stock grant. It was an exciting amount of money, but I was mostly thrilled to be called into Lou's office and to have him recognize my work. Oddly, one thing that sticks out in my mind from that experience was Lou's comments on my wardrobe. Over the years, I had adopted business suits as my preferred attire, and on that day, I was wearing a pair of women's wing tips. Lou was fascinated by a woman wearing men's-style shoes without any socks.

In general, I was captivated by Lou's instincts and grasp of the technology business. I also admired his passion for customers. I started spending a lot of time in Armonk, New York, as higher-level executives increasingly took notice and started getting involved in our business. I would often see Lou bustling around the halls and he would never say a word to anyone or indicate that he knew who you might be. One day, however, I invited the founder and Chief Technology Officer (CTO) of Juniper Networks, Pradeep Sindhu, to an early morning meeting in Armonk. I was strolling into the building with Pradeep at the same time Lou was arriving at work. Lou immediately sensed that Pradeep was a customer and came right over to say hello, greeting me by name. I introduced them, and Lou started probing Pradeep about his business and invited him to his office, where they had an animated discussion about communications and networking. I enjoyed making that connection and watching the result.

Things were going great, but with my business growing so rapidly, it was becoming an impossible task to manage the entire P&L all by myself, so I spoke with John, and we decided to break the Wired Communications group up into its three natural technology subunits—Custom Logic/ASICs, Network Processors, and Transport—and to share the P&L responsibility. If you're leading a large enterprise, you have to know when (and be able) to delegate responsibility clearly to your team. The tight group I started with to develop the strategy and plan was great, but executing the plan would require leaving behind the "wearing multiple hats" phase of our business and the adoption of clear individual responsibilities. And we would need leaders well-suited to those responsibilities. I chose David Balkin and eventually one of my former critics, Tom Reeves, to manage our primary Custom Logic business, which was a more mature, high-volume business better aligned to IBM's typical processes and operations. Although Tom had been a major naysayer, I knew he would be skilled at managing a mature business and that he would provide a sense of stability for our customers. I chose Jim Northington to run our "growth" business of Network Processors, and Dale Chris to run our "emerging" Transport business. Both of those businesses were unlike any other businesses at IBM and would require leaders with unique skill sets and risk-taking personalities like mine. Working with these leaders, we were positioned to continue our rapid pace of growth. This structural evolution would inspire a Harvard Business School case study as a result of my conversations with a professor during one of IBM's managerial training programs (I'll share more on the case study and its impact on my career later in this chapter).

As we got to the height of the dot com boom, our products were so in demand that I found myself facing the challenge of having *too much* business. I suppose some companies would like to have that sort of "problem," but not being able to deliver the products our customers needed and counted on was exceedingly upsetting for me. There were just not enough materials to satisfy all the packaging and silicon needs of our customers. There were shortages everywhere. All of our major customers were screaming for more parts, and our supply constraints were placing our startup customers at existential risk. "I've invested my life in this and now you're saying I can't grow," said one of the many CEOs who came to my office panicked and on the verge of tears. I remember one time Compaq's CEO went so far as to send a jet to pick up 30 parts that controlled the timing on Dell's high-end computers. Customers large and small were all clamoring for parts. The CEOs of HP, Cisco, and anyone else who could get hold of Lou Gerstner were calling him to try to get more components, but Lou was a real team player. He always asked them, "Do you know Chris King? Talk to her. I know she will do her best to take care of you." So, every CEO in the industry was calling me, and I quickly became extremely popular, although not necessarily in the manner I would have liked. Eventually, thanks to our extraordinary efforts to expand capacity (and the dot com crash's impact on customer demand), we were able to get things under control, but it wasn't easy. As David Balkin said about that time, "It was probably the worst part of my life."[6] Being as customer-centric as I am, I can't help but agree with David's assessment.

By the summer of 2000, Jim Vanderslice left IBM to join Dell as their Vice Chairman. John Kelly was promoted to replace Jim as Technology Group executive, leaving a vacuum in the Microelectronics GM role. We were all wondering who would be selected as the new GM, and in my heart of hearts I hoped and thought I would be the best choice.

Then, in August, I got the call from John that I was going to be promoted! But it was for a newly created role—Vice President (VP) of Semiconductor Solutions—not the GM of the Microelectronics division role I was hoping for. John explained that they were splitting the GM role into two roles; one focused on semiconductor products and the other focused on manufacturing and operations. I was crestfallen. I was given the more critical role, overseeing about 8000 people across the five business lines that John Kelly had previously managed, as well as product development and engineering (so much for Jim Picciano's threat that I would never be able to come back to development!) and the P&L, which at the time was about $6 billion—but I still felt cheated. John said they had split it that way so I could concentrate on growing the business by leaning into my strengths in strategy and customers and delegating the minutiae to others, but it *felt* like they didn't trust me to run the whole division.

They gave manufacturing and operations to Doug Grose. I really liked Doug as he was a down-to-earth guy and great at what he did, but he was also much more conservative in his risk-taking than I was. I knew that might be a problem down the line as we tried to work together to achieve the division's goals, but at that time I didn't realize *how* challenging it would end up being.

Others seemed to, though. At our first large management meeting in front of the hundreds of division managers, they presented a skit about our differing styles. As the action began, "I" was sitting in an office, and Cisco called me because they needed a new product designed and built on a very abbreviated schedule. In response, the person playing me kept saying, "Sure we can do that! No problem!" over and over. After she got off the call with Cisco, she left and went to Doug's office to tell him what we had to do. He of course responded, "NO!! We can't do that!!!" over and over. The skit got a really big laugh, because, of course, it was true.

Thinking back on the decision to give Doug manufacturing, though, I realize that the manufacturing team may have resented the fact that I hadn't followed the traditional path up the ladder and had taken some "shortcuts" in my irreverent manner. John and the other leaders may have thought manufacturing would resist my leadership if they didn't break things up. If I *had* followed the traditional path, however, I'm fairly sure I never would have gotten to a position where it was an issue, because it was the risks I took and untrodden paths I chose that allowed me to outperform my peers and rise to the position of being considered for the GM of Microelectronics position.

I was also surprised to not be "promoted" from my cubicle to an office. When John had the role I now had, he had been given an office, which made it much easier to work the tremendous number of hours and have the types of conversations the role required. As I have said before, I try not to "sweat the small stuff," but in this case, it wasn't really about comfort and status. Being in a cubicle affected the way people saw me, and it was important that they saw me as the boss, so I made my case to John and was able to get an office. It wasn't a glamorous office, but it did the trick. That said, when I traveled from my primary office in Fishkill to Burlington to meet with roughly one-third of my employees, the local staff stuck me in a small cubicle. I wasn't even given the respect that would be afforded to a lower-level manager. When John Kelly had been the division head, everyone had tripped over themselves to make him comfortable. Even though those same people now worked for me, I found myself relegated to a cubicle without any fanfare. Were they sending a message? Some of those managers who reported to me in Burlington had corner offices, and thinking back on it, I should have made them come to my cubicle for our meetings!

Office trappings aside, the financial and other benefits were starting to roll in. Beyond salary and bonus increases and stock grants, I started representing IBM at high-profile, interesting events. For example, IBM had always been a main sponsor for the Olympics and used that sponsorship as an opportunity to entertain and bond with customers. I had never been chosen to attend an event like that, but now I was the head of the division and had all of the customer responsibility, so I was selected to go to the 2000 Sydney Olympics. What an amazing experience!

I remember that hotel space was limited that year, so I had a room in a cruise ship that IBM had rented and moored in the Sydney harbor next to the Opera House and across from the Harbour Bridge. My friend Dr. Kin, whom I had first met when he managed sales for John Gleason in Asia and Japan and who was now the head of sales for the Microelectronics division, had the room next to mine. We were working around the clock to meet the insatiable demand for our semiconductor solutions, and Dr. Kin told me he could hear me through our shared wall at all hours explaining to customers when they would get their parts. Being stuck in my stateroom managing upset customers wasn't how I had envisioned attending the Olympics. When I finally got out of my room and was taking a launch across the harbor to see the Games, a customer on a launch headed the other way screamed at me across the water that he needed more parts! Fortunately, I was only responsible for entertaining a small group of customers from the US and Europe at the Olympics, and once we got over the first day's discussions about where their parts were, we had a wonderful time!

In terms of my role, I now had responsibility for all of IBM Microelectronics' semiconductor products as well as all development and design. It was a big job and I jumped into it with enthusiasm. I wanted to spend lots of time with customers, but also with my new, very large team, and on top of that, I had many, many reviews with John and Lou.

At this point, I had been living out of a suitcase for a few years. John Gleason had established the Sales headquarters in Boston, so I rented an apartment there while I was working for him and came home to Vermont every weekend. When I started working for John Kelly, my office moved to Fishkill, New York, and I traveled to Armonk and Somers often. I stayed in hotels for a while, but that got old, so I rented a small, local carriage house that had been converted into an apartment. I was traveling a lot, but fortunately Eric had finished college and was working as a media designer in Minneapolis, and Megan was in her twenties and attending Brandeis University, so Jack was the only one left at home (and I think he kind of liked the peace and quiet!). Of course, I still tried to make it home every weekend to make the most of my time with Jack and the kids when they were around.

That first year running my division was a whirlwind, though. My office was jumping, and I was receiving 300–500 emails every day! I had two great administrative assistants to keep my calendar straight, arrange my travel, and find the various things I lost in hotels, cars, and planes. I also hired two technical assistants who helped me with everything, including my many presentations (they also got stuck with trying to manage my email, only routing critical items to me).

One of my technical assistants was Sumit Sadana. I received a call from him shortly after I got my job. He was a first-line manager from the server group, and he said that running a computer-design group was getting boring and that he wanted to be where the action was (he had heard that I was where the action was). Sumit really learned his stuff, and at the time of this writing he is an executive vice president (EVP) at Micron, one of the world's larger memory makers and semiconductor companies.

My small staff and I worked from sunrise to late at night reporting to management, spending time with customers, managing the development engineering team, cajoling the manufacturing team, and so on. I often left for my little carriage apartment at two or three in the morning. It was a full-time job just to juggle the parts we could manufacture to keep our customers' production lines from shutting down. That made it hard to hunt for the new customers and business our management (and I) expected!

One of the challenging aspects of my new role was that many of my old bosses now worked for me. I was sensitive to the fact that the tables had turned, but it was still my job to get the most out of these executives. My very first manager at IBM, Bob Fiorenza, was now part of my reporting structure. Ken Torino, who had famously said that I was a great lieutenant but would never be a general, was now several levels below me, as were Bruce Beers, Tom Reeves, and Hank Geipel. I was now in a position to make or break the careers of these executives, individuals who hadn't always been kind to me on my way up, but my motto is to always do the right thing. So, I took any personal feelings out of play when making decisions. I kept as my North Star the belief that the customer was the center of everything we did, and that guided my management of former bosses. For example, my old boss Hank had the trademark IBM arrogance and had difficulty listening to and complying with customers' needs. Qualcomm, the startup that no one had wanted me to work with originally, was now a huge customer and Hank was in charge of their business. The Qualcomm leaders told me in no uncertain terms they did not want to see him in their offices, so I had Hank focus on what he was best at—manufacturing and making sure we had enough parts as Qualcomm's mobile phone business grew like gangbusters— while I managed the customer-facing role. Customers have always been my passion, so picking up that responsibility was less an added obligation and more a welcome opportunity to do the type of work I most enjoy.

As the year flipped over to 2001, it was clear that the dot com boom was running out of steam. I recognized that it was critical to closely align our new products and projects to our customers' needs so we could keep our revenue growing, but even with our best efforts, the writing was on the wall that revenue growth would be extremely challenging. I was also responsible for profitability beyond top-line revenue growth, and our manufacturing costs were a big part of that. This would be the area in which Doug Grose's and my conflicting styles would start to create issues.

I was an old hand at keeping development costs in line, but manufacturing costs were another animal altogether and they were under Doug's control. I started to visit Doug in his office on a regular basis to discuss how we could reduce our cost of manufacturing. I kept brainstorming ideas; for example, I suggested keeping our equipment in service longer, rather than always splurging on the latest equipment advances for everything we made. I recognized that manufacturing is complex and that it was all new to me, but I was certain that together we could figure out how to get our costs in line. Doug was very polite and listened to me, but since he wasn't responsible for the P&L, I'm not sure he took any of my ideas seriously or pursued them any further.

These emerging challenges aside, the year started with a feather in my cap when Lou Gerstner invited me to speak to the top 200 leaders at IBM at the 2001 Senior Leadership Conference in Florida in March (a welcome break from the late winter of New York!). Over the course of my career, I had delivered speeches using an outline on a few small cards at most. I thought "winging it" allowed me to be natural and have my enthusiasm come through. This speech was different, however, and particularly important to me since it was an opportunity to demonstrate my leadership style and its results to *all* of IBM. The speech was so important that I actually wrote out every word and memorized the script so I wouldn't inadvertently leave out any of the good parts. I focused my talk on how to "create" a great business, because after all, who else besides me had ever really done that at IBM? Well, maybe Sam Palmisano, who is credited with starting IBM's Services business.

It was quite a rush when I took the stage. The lights in my face were bright, but I could see Lou Gerstner, CFO John Joyce, General Counsel Larry Ricciardi, and President and Chief Operations Officer (and future CEO) Sam Palmisano in the front row. I couldn't see him, but I also knew my friend Dr. Kin was in the audience. I started my speech and within the first 60 seconds I knew that I had them in the palm of my hand. My experience starting and running Expedition Electronics immediately hooked the audience and they were amazed and amused at the thought of me waiting at the mailbox for the checks from my customers that would allow us to keep the lights on and keep innovating and growing. The story of how I launched and grew the ASIC business was an eye-opener for them. I took the high road, of course, in terms of the internal challenges and setbacks I had encountered from my managers and others, but my wry sense of humor about the experience and focus on our customers got a lot of laughs and about as much applause as one can get from a room full of 200 people. Everyone came up to me after the speech, gushing over my performance. I got plenty of compliments and felt like a real star. I had completely blown the room away with all that my teams and I had accomplished over the years! I will forever remember that speech and experience.

By the second quarter of 2001, we had emptied the backlog of demand for parts that had kept us running hot as the dot com crash accelerated. I knew it was going to be incredibly challenging to achieve the more than $1 billion in revenue we had committed to, but I felt we could do it. Once again, I worked around the clock with Dr. Kin to make sure we had the sales to reach our goals, and by the time June 30th and the end of the quarter arrived, we knew we had done it! We made our target by the skin of our teeth, but we had done it.

I went into the July 4th weekend feeling great. I had planned a week off, cruising Lake Champlain in Vermont in our new Formula 382 Fastech cigarette boat, *Out of the Blue*.[7] Early in the week, we went to lunch with some of Jack's family and were enjoying ourselves immensely when my cell phone rang with a call from my office. They confirmed that yes, we had made our revenue target, but our manufacturing costs were so high for the quarter that we had missed our bottom-line target by many millions of dollars. I was crushed and, frankly, a little angry.

The manufacturing costs were killing our profitability despite my best efforts to convince Doug and his gigantic organization to do things differently to keep costs under control. I went back to the office on July 9th, resolved to work as hard as I could to make our numbers, but I couldn't escape the sickening feeling that I was engaged in an unwinnable, Sisyphean task. I just didn't see how I could get Doug and his team to do what was needed to hit our profitability goals in the new quarter, and I didn't see that prospect changing at any point in the future. I started to wonder if this might be one of those times when I needed to take my own advice, "When you can't go through, go around." But at this point in my career, the only way "around" would be out. Out of IBM.

By this time, my success was well known in the industry, and publications were calling me the most powerful woman in semiconductors. Headhunters were calling on an almost daily basis, but I didn't take their calls since they were usually calling about CEO positions at smaller startups, which didn't really interest me. To keep my options open, though, Jack volunteered to be my agent, and my office began to route these calls to him for screening.

As fate would have it, one day during that first week back after the holiday, Jack called me and said he had a call from a recruiter about a CEO opportunity with a company called AMI Semiconductor. I had never heard of AMI Semiconductor, but Jack said it sounded interesting and that I should talk to them. *Well, if Jack thought it sounded interesting*, I thought to myself, *it just might be!*

I gave the guy a call. He explained that the role would be leading the former American Microsystems (now renamed AMI Semiconductor), an old semiconductor company that had been larger than Intel in the 1970s but had languished under the ownership of a Japanese energy company since then. The recruiter wanted to meet with me to discuss the role, but given my schedule, finding time for a meeting was nearly impossible. I was booked in wall-to-wall meetings and commitments for months, so I told him I could meet him at 6:00 a.m. at a little diner about 35 minutes away on the Taconic Parkway for a breakfast meeting, which would allow me to get back to the office by 7:30. He agreed. So, at 5:25 a.m., I jumped into my red M5 BMW and hopped on the Taconic Parkway to drive to the meeting. On the way, though, the pressures of the day started to weigh on me and I began to question whether the meeting was a good idea. I was way too busy to be taking time out of my IBM schedule to chase some opportunity, so I called Jack to say I was going to turn around, but he said, "Hey, you're already in the car! What's an hour or two out of your schedule to check it out?" So, I kept going.

When I met the recruiter, he said that the company had just been acquired by two private equity firms. He reiterated its long history and the fact that it was located in Pocatello, Idaho (*Where on earth is that?!* I thought to myself). The company seemed to be asleep at the wheel and was losing money, but they primarily developed ASICs, which piqued my interest (even though they sure didn't have IBM's sophistication). At the time, I had more than $4 million in unvested IBM stock (including the $1 million award that Lou had given me in his office), and so I told the recruiter that before we went any further, they would need to make me whole if I came on board. He said that might not be a problem since the private equity firms had just paid $360 million for the company and didn't have anyone to run it. They needed me. I left the meeting feeling that Jack had been right. It was an interesting opportunity and something worth exploring further.

The next week I had a series of customer meetings in the Bay Area, where one of the private equity firms, Francisco Partners, happened to also be based. They asked if I could stop by and meet them and I agreed, but I realized I didn't have a résumé to give them. Since I hadn't been looking to leave IBM, I hadn't bothered to put one together. I did, however, have a killer Harvard Business School case study,[8] the one I mentioned earlier about my work at IBM building its Wired Communications business. Figuring that not everyone has a Harvard Business School case study, I decided to give that to the partners in lieu of a résumé.

The case study was the result of IBM's terrific manager and executive education program. From the time I was appointed to my first manager job (and with every subsequent promotion), IBM had sent me to a week of leadership training at the IBM Educational Development Center in Armonk, New York. In time, the training expanded to two weeks, and then at my current level we had the opportunity to learn from professors at Stanford and Harvard. I loved it. Not only did it give us a chance to "get out of the weeds" and think about our roles and future, but it was also great to meet, network with, and learn from other IBM executives.

So, I got to attend Harvard for two weeks of mini MBA training, and it was there that I met and got to know Michael Tushman, a renowned professor at the Harvard Business School. The trip had an ominous start—my wallet was stolen in Grand Central Station on the way to Boston—but the Harvard trip ended up being one of those critical moments in my career.

Michael led the class and discussion about various strategies for running complex businesses. He seemed to take a lot of interest in my career, how I had successfully managed IBM's Wired Communications business, and how I allocated investments between our more mature Core product groups, our Growth groups, and our Emerging groups. He asked if he could do a Harvard Business School case study describing our business, its challenges, and how we addressed them. At the time I didn't really think anything would come of it, but I appreciated the conversation and was thrilled by the possibility. I was surprised when IBM agreed to the case study, and before I knew it, Michael, his colleagues, and a professor from Stanford embarked on what would be a year-long project interviewing many of those involved in our Wired Communications business. When I read their draft of the case study, I couldn't help but laugh. I was so pleased! It was a great piece of work and described our efforts perfectly.

When I arrived at Francisco Partners, I handed my case study to the partner, Dipanjan "DJ" Deb, and said, "I think this does a pretty good job of describing my leadership style and accomplishments." I was immediately struck that this young man was barely 30 years old—these guys were so young! We had a great conversation and he said he wanted to pursue me as a candidate for the AMI Semiconductor CEO role. He asked me if I could meet the other partners in New York City, and since my office was only an hour away, I thought, *Why not?* The next week I went to the Four Seasons on 57th Street in New York to meet Chip Schorr for breakfast, this time at 8:00 a.m., since I was more interested now and making more time to pursue the opportunity. When I walked into the hotel to meet Chip, I was astounded once again to be facing a young man who was also barely 30. They were both very smart guys, though, and obviously knew what they were doing.

During the meeting, I made it clear that I needed a guarantee that they would cover the amount I would be leaving on the table at IBM if I were to leave. When they said they would find a way to work it out, I realized this could really happen!

As it turns out, they had interviewed almost 50 executives for the position, but after our two meetings, the recruiter called me and said that I was one of the two finalists for the position! He asked if I could travel to Pocatello to meet the executive team. I had a lot of saved-up vacation, and Jack and I both loved the West. We had never really been to Idaho and so it would be both a job interview and an adventure! In early August, we flew into Salt Lake City and drove north to Pocatello. Pocatello reminded me of our rural Vermont home, but with a Wild Wild West twist, and I loved it! I had a round of interviews with the senior executives at the company. It was clear that they did not have the technology or innovation DNA that IBM was steeped in, but they were a going entity and I started to imagine what I might be able to accomplish there. The leadership team wasn't quite where I would have liked it to be, but there did appear to be some diamonds in the rough that I would be able to develop and rely on.

While the location was beautiful and the meetings with the senior leadership team had gone well, I was still on the fence about leaving IBM. I had accomplished so much there. And IBM was the premier technology company on the leading edge of *everything*. AMI Semiconductor was basically on the other end of the spectrum — small, far from "the action," and underperforming in the market. After the day was over and we were pulling out of the parking lot, though, I looked back at the buildings and thought to myself, *I could be in charge of this WHOLE thing!* I had long wanted to be a CEO someday, and this was my chance. It was also just the sort of opportunity I loved—a solid but underperforming company (which included an ASIC business) that had been neglected and only needed consistent, effective leadership to achieve its full potential. If I took the role, there would be no one above me (except, of course, the owners and Board of Directors) and the buck would stop with me. I started to get really excited! The idea of being the leader shaping and reforming the business was exactly what I had wanted, so as I looked back at those buildings, I could feel the future before me starting to fall into place.

As it turned out, the owners envisioned the same future. After my visit to the site, DJ and Chip heard that the team thought I was the best choice. They called and offered me the job, which would make me the first female CEO of a semiconductor company![9]

At the time, female CEOs of sizeable technology companies were almost unheard of. Carly Fiorina had become the first female CEO of a large technology company when she became the leader of Hewlett-Packard just two years earlier! I was proud to be part of this early cadre of female CEOs, but honestly, being a "first" was never my goal. I just enjoyed creating great businesses; "breaking glass ceilings" was always secondary. That said, I did recognize my responsibility to be a role model to the other women who would follow me. IBM had a woman's executive career development initiative, and while a number of the young female engineers and managers participated and provided support, I rarely had the time to do so and always felt guilty because I knew how hard being a woman executive is. When I finally did go to a meeting the whole group chorused, "We don't need you here! Please just continue doing what you're doing! You are breaking ground for us and that is the best thing you can do!" That felt nice to hear, and this book is one of the ways I hope that I am continuing to help women to accelerate their careers and achieve even more than I have.

My financial negotiations with DJ and Chip to close the deal were interesting. They were happy to give me the bonus I requested for leaving so much money on the table at IBM,[10] and DJ said I was asking for too little money in my base salary and bumped it up $50,000 more! I felt very wanted and supported by my new bosses!

The next step would be telling IBM that I was leaving. DJ and Chip said they wanted me to resist the undoubtable pressure that IBM would apply to get me to stay. They said they were there for me if I wanted to talk at any point during the leaving process. When I got back to New York, it broke my heart to tell John Kelly that I was leaving. I think he understood, and he was very gracious about it, but it was still hard. I think that Lou Gerstner was disappointed. He asked Sam Palmisano to try to talk me into staying. Amazingly, they tried to get me to stay by offering me the head of sales position for the Technology Group. They didn't get me at all! I wanted to be in charge of a business end-to-end; not sales, no matter how big it was. Sam asked me to imagine myself sitting in the IBM boardroom, because he assumed it would be the dream of everyone to sit in the IBM boardroom, but I was thinking to myself, *No, I can't imagine sitting in that room when I could be out building a business and making it happen!* He was trying to make any argument stick, but I finally said, "I have always wanted to be a cowgirl and I can do that in Pocatello, Idaho."

He gulped and responded, "Well, to that I have no answer!"

Later, as I began packing up my office, I was surprised to not be more sad to be leaving IBM, the company in which I had spent 23 years of my life and where I had been shaped into the executive I had become. I was just too excited to start my new adventure at AMI Semiconductor. As I carefully put books, awards, and other trinkets in boxes and looked around my increasingly bare office, though, I couldn't help but reflect on the journey that had brought me to this moment. There had been many twists and turns since that gas station moment, when I looked out into the bleak night hoping for "some way out of here." And now, I would be the first female CEO of a semiconductor company and sitting in *my own* boardroom (and there would be many more boardrooms in my future). I smiled to myself as I thought about my circuitous path, with all of its setbacks and highs and lows, and how, through it all, I had never given up and never stopped moving, whether it was up, sideways, or down. The trick is to keep exploring, discovering, and experiencing this wonderful world in which we live.

Lesson #11—Everyone Loves Results

If there is anything more important than the power of the customer, which I mentioned in Lesson #9, it's the power of results. Most people have a vision for their life and careers. Most people can imagine a path to achieving their visions. But those who can walk that path successfully are few. It's like they say, if success were easy, everyone would have it. It is because of the difficulty of delivering results that those who are able to achieve them are recognized, respected, and rewarded.

In the business world, the results that matter most are financial results. Everything else in the business is secondary, since, as I have mentioned before, revenue and profits are the lifeblood of any organization. At the end of the day, the effectiveness and efficiency of everything you do—from setting and executing a strategy, to working with customers, to getting the most out of the team—manifests itself in financial results. Financial results reflect the value your effort has created, from how much someone is willing to pay for it, to how well you have delivered it through your operations.

So, as difficult as focusing on the customer is, it is actually easier than focusing on results. When you're focused on the customer, you can be single-minded. Your customers' success is all that really matters, and you can operate with that single goal in mind. Financial results require balancing multiple goals to deliver optimized, organization-wide results.

I began to truly understand this when I was running IBM's Wired business and was responsible for the full P&L for the first time. Our customers were still our focus, but they became one piece of a larger puzzle I was working to solve. As challenging as that would be normally, the hypergrowth time period we were living through meant that there was never enough capacity or resources and we had to be creative to continue meeting the needs of our customers without breaking the bank. Even if we could have built or bought additional capacity, you can't do so if it destroys your margins and lowers your overall financial results. I had to figure out how to deliver a complete package of financial results—revenue growth *and* profitability.

That's why I found my final role at IBM, VP of Semiconductor Solutions, so frustrating. I had *responsibility* for the full P&L, but not *control* over the critical levers in manufacturing that would dictate my ultimate P&L success or failure. I killed myself to deliver the top-line revenue growth that was expected, but still failed to deliver the complete financial results because I didn't fully control the bottom line. That lack of control of the mechanisms underlying our financial results is why I finally left IBM.

I thrive in a world of results, because they are so concrete and tangible. People can smooth-talk and finesse just about anything in the business world, but you can't do that with results. Either you delivered them, or you didn't. You can't argue with results, just like you can't fake the amount of milk in the bucket when milking a cow.

Many of you reading this book probably do not have full P&L responsibility (not yet at least!), but you can still apply this lesson in your lives by staying focused on delivering financial results in whatever you are doing. Whether you're a CEO or the fry guy at McDonald's, the financial results you deliver are what matter. If you can make your fries so that customers love how hot, crispy, and salty they are and keep coming back for more, and if you can do it in less time and with less waste than before, your managers will notice, and rewards should follow, because everyone loves results.

Lesson #12—Always Do the Right Thing

Throughout this book, I've spoken about having North Stars—a business's mission, customer success, financial results—but it is also important to have a moral compass to guide you on the journey. In business, there are numerous opportunities to *not* do the right thing, under the guise of pursuing some supposedly greater goal. There are opportunities to fib to a customer to secure a better deal. There are opportunities to misrepresent the truth to a manager to buy yourself more time to correct a situation. There are opportunities to mistreat those around you, either to gain leverage or, in my case, to right past wrongs. Not doing the right thing, though, never works out in the long run. Customers will recognize that you are not trustworthy and stop doing business with you. Managers will adapt to your dishonesty and treat you accordingly. And you never know which butts you kicked today you will have to kiss tomorrow.

IBM believed it was the industry's 800-pound gorilla, that it could dictate onerous rules of engagement with its customers, and that customers should just be happy to be working with IBM. I never saw it that way. That struck me as the way to put yourself out of business. Instead, I always worked to find a path to win-win agreements, where both IBM and the customer felt like it was a good deal. It was an example of doing the right thing, even when you didn't have to. And the result was that I built some of IBM's most successful businesses on a foundation of incredible customer loyalty.

When I found myself in the situation of being able to exact retribution on previous managers who hadn't treated me fairly, it never really appealed to me. It just wasn't worth my time, and it certainly wasn't worth lowering myself to that level. I had built a reputation for always doing the right thing and that's why people wanted to work with me, even if they didn't necessarily like me. I remember a conversation I once had with the CEO of TSMC North America where he said, "A lot of people don't like you, but they all say you are always fair and do the right thing and that's why they work with you." People are attracted to honesty and integrity. In this world, doing the right thing is revolutionary and will set you apart.

That's not to say that doing the right thing is always easy. In fact, it can be downright painful sometimes. For example, I always found doing the right thing with a poor performer on my team to be challenging. I don't like to hurt people, but when people are poor performers, even after you have taken the time to help them improve, you have to move them out. It's the right thing for the team and for them. There's nothing more demoralizing for a team of high performers than to see their manager tolerate a poor performer. And for that poor performer, nudging them out is the right thing too. They might not see it at the time, but poor performance is usually a result of someone being a poor fit for a role, and it's better for them to leave and find a better fit where they will be happier and succeed.

Ultimately, it comes down to setting aside your ego and feelings in favor of a larger mission and accomplishing something greater than yourself. When you set your ego aside, it frees you to do the right thing and accomplish far more than you could otherwise. And taking the high road, like anything you practice, becomes easier over time. You start out doing the right thing once or twice and it either works out well or the consequences are not as bad as you feared. More often than not, it will work out for the best, so have faith. And those little successes will compound upon themselves, giving you the confidence to do the right thing again the next time. Eventually, doing the right thing becomes second nature.

And when that happens, beyond being differentiated in your career, you will be differentiated in life!

Notes

1   Wood, Robert Chapman and Michael L. Tushman, "IBM Network Technology (A)," p. 8, Harvard Business School Publishing, 2001

2   Wood and Tushman, "IBM Network Technology (A)," p. 8

3   Wood and Tushman, "IBM Network Technology (A)," p. 12

4   Wood and Tushman, "IBM Network Technology (A)," p. 10

5   Fortunately, there were leaders at IBM, like Lou Gerstner, Jim Vanderslice, and John Kelly, who weren't thoroughly enamored with the IBM way. They valued results and recognized that whether my way was the IBM way or not, I got results. They probably raised an eyebrow or two over the years at how I did things, but they always supported me.

6   Wood and Tushman, "IBM Network Technology (A)," p. 15

7   We had christened our new boat *Out of the Blue* because we had used the money I had earned at IBM (Big Blue), the decision to purchase the boat came from "out of the blue," and of course, water is blue.

8   Wood, Robert Chapman and Michael L. Tushman, "IBM Network Technology (A&B)," Harvard Business School Publishing, 2001

9   In an *Electronic Business* article in September 2002, DJ was asked about hiring me as the first female CEO of a semiconductor company. He responded that he didn't even know that had been the case and that he had never thought about it. "She was just far and away the best-qualified candidate."

10 Since AMI was a private company that was losing money, I asked DJ and Chip to leave the bonus money in an escrow account that I could draw upon if the AMI stock didn't pan out. As it turned out, I made so much money with the AMI stock, they never had to pay me the $4.2 million bonus!

Epilogue

September 2001

The weeks after resigning from IBM were a whirlwind. I was sad to leave the many friends I had made over the years, but I was mostly looking forward to my next adventure as a CEO, the first female CEO in the semiconductor industry.

I took two weeks off before starting at AMI to enjoy a vacation on Lake Champlain with Jack, my kids, and my parents (who were happy that their "wayward" daughter had become such a success!). Then, on September 10, 2001, I boarded a flight to San Francisco to meet with Tom Epley, who was the acting CEO of AMI. I arrived in the early afternoon, and we immediately boarded his private plane to fly to Pocatello. I thought, *Wow! I could get used to this private jet travel!* We reviewed the AMI executives during the flight to Pocatello. There seemed to be some issues, which wasn't a surprise given the company's current situation, but there also seemed to be some good talent on the team. We planned to have dinner with the senior leadership team that evening, and then spend the next day reviewing the business from top to bottom.[1]

The dinner that night was very cordial, and I enjoyed meeting everyone. I was the new boss, so everyone was very deferential to me, which was so different from anything else I had experienced in my career.

I got up early the next morning to start my first day as CEO. As I got ready in my hotel room, I switched on the news and was shocked to see smoke billowing from the North Tower of the World Trade Center. I picked up my cell phone to call my parents and ask what was going on since they lived right across the river. They weren't sure, but as I was speaking with them, a plane hit the South Tower and we all knew something dreadful was happening. I called Jack, who was in Vermont packing things up to ship to Idaho. I had planned to return to Vermont to finish packing up and taking care of some last-minute issues later that day, but that of course wasn't going to happen now.

I was glued to the TV, but I knew I needed to get to the office. Once I arrived, I discovered that people in Idaho didn't seem quite as concerned as I was about the morning's events because New York was so far away for them. I quickly asked if they had a television set so I could catch up on what was happening. They found a TV in security that they wheeled down to the conference room in which we were meeting. I remember the reception was terrible. We all gathered for the initial introductory meeting, but it was hard to keep focused and I kept asking for breaks so I could go see what was happening.

When the third plane crashed into the Pentagon and the South Tower fell, even the folks in Idaho recognized the seriousness of the situation. Tom Epley took the company car and hightailed it to his place in the Colorado Mountains. I immediately went to the airport to get the best rental car I could find in case I had to drive somewhere (it was clear no one would be flying anytime soon). I only had one carry-on bag with a single change of clothes. I was about to find out how difficult it was to find women's business suits in Pocatello, Idaho. I was pretty shaken up and feeling very isolated from home and everyone I knew on the other side of the country. I was beginning a new chapter of my life in many ways—new career, new home—but those so negatively impacted on September 11th weighed heavily on me.

My new secretary, Kelly, asked if I would like to move into the temporary apartment they had for me instead of staying in the hotel, which seemed like a good move that might help inject some normalcy into what was happening. It turned out that the apartment was on a hill that overlooked the AMI facility. In the dark that night, when the world seemed to be falling apart, I looked down on the AMI buildings with their big red and blue AMIS logo sign illuminating the night, and I found some peace.

Speaking of peace, and issues of faith, which I came to find played more and more of a role in my life as my career progressed, Jack had included some personal pictures for me in the shipment he was packing at the exact time he learned of the 9/11 attack. Somehow, that package managed to get to me several days later. To my amazement, when I opened the large box, the first thing I saw was a picture of me and my family on Ellis Island with the Twin Towers in the background. For whatever reason, the picture and the serendipity of its arrival at that moment seemed like a sign that I was in the right place and doing the right thing.

When people asked me if it was hard being a CEO in a new company after working at IBM my whole career, I responded, "No, it's exactly the same. It's still all about the customers, the team, the strategy, and the execution. It's just smaller." Don't get me wrong. There were new challenges and things to learn, like the world of finance and capital markets, which was all new to me. I spent countless hours sitting with my Chief Financial Officer and Wall Street bankers in those early weeks and months wondering what they were talking about. GAAP accounting, equity positions, company valuation, basis points—it went on and on. But I sat there and listened, absorbing everything they said and not letting on that I was clueless. I thought to myself, *I figured out how to build a computer and milk a cow. How hard could finance be?!*

AMI was already losing money and the revenue dropped significantly after 9/11. We soldiered on and in 2002 I had the opportunity to acquire Alcatel Microelectronics, which was owned by a French company, located in Belgium, and also losing money. I was able to negotiate a chance to combine a "seat of the pants" American company with a "precise but slow" European company. I committed to taking the *best* of both companies to create a new, solid company, and we were able to return to profitability within the year.

I hired some of my old friends from IBM like Ann Rincon, Darlene Gerry, and Mike O'Neill. My initial sense that some of the Pocatello executives would not work well with my management style turned out to be correct, but there were definitely some diamonds in the rough and I promoted those people.

All of this led to our successful initial public offering (IPO) in September of 2003, which was almost as exciting as starting the ASIC business at IBM earlier in my career. It was a $600 million IPO and made DJ and Chip, who had hired me, *very* happy! Now I had a new set of public company investors, many of whom would end up following me and investing in the companies with which I was involved in the years to come. My new mantra became "customers, team, and owners!"

While there continued to be pitfalls and the occasional backward steps, I was persistent in moving forward and completing the mission, just as I had done for my entire life. I had finally arrived in the position where the buck stopped with me. I was the one in charge and able to develop an environment of success for my customers and owners, and most of all, for my team of several thousand.

For me, it was and always has been about building something great—something that had not been there before, whether a company, a career, or an avocation. None of us knows what comes next after we die, so make the most of your time here to do something great with your life and for the world!

Semiconductors' leading lady takes helm

BY TERRY COSTLOW

Christine King's life is taking another unexpected turn this week as she becomes the CEO of AMI Semiconductor Inc. But surprising twists aren't uncommon for the engineer who previously headed IBM Microelectronics' business. King says she studiously avoided technology in high school, and she was a welfare mother when she took her first engineering class to impress a boyfriend.

King was an integral part of IBM's efforts to enter the merchant IC market during the 1990s, and she had enough success to rise swiftly to vice president of IBM Semiconductor Products. "I always figure that as long as IBM gives me entrepreneurial jobs, I'm very happy here," King said a few weeks before announcing she would leave Big Blue to run AMI Semiconductor.

"I wasn't anticipating leaving IBM, but when the opportunity came to my attention, I was very interested," King told *EE Times* just before Labor Day, while driving her parents to her new home in Pocatello, Idaho, where AMIS is headquartered.

Thirty-five-year-old AMIS isn't exactly a startup, but with revenue of less than $400 million last year, the privately held company has but a fraction of IBM's estimated $3.5 billion in revenue, a sum that doesn't include substantial captive shipments. But for King, the chance to take the top spot in Idaho was more enticing than running an IBM division in New York.

"I always aspired to be a CEO," King said. "I really wanted to lead an entire company. I love entrepreneurial ventures. This is a great opportunity to lead a company with a lot of potential. I want to make it a leading force in the market."

She defined "leading force" as "being a leader in your chosen markets and having top-of-the-line growth, being profitable." For AMIS, ASICs represent the key for those chosen markets.

"I think one of the strengths of AMI is its ASIC capabilities," King said. "Some of the areas I'm excited about are their strengths in analog mixed-signal, which I've always seen as a hot market. I'm also impressed with the work they do converting FPGAs and programmable logic into lower-cost, higher-density solutions."

Asked whether her game plan might include an acquisition, King was noncommittal. "That's always a possibility everywhere. I wouldn't rule it out, but I haven't started my first day there yet," she said.

At IBM, King became one of the most powerful women in the chip business. She rose to the vice presidential level in 1998, becoming VP of worldwide marketing and field engineering, then, in 1999, vice president of wired communications. She assumed her most recent job in April 2000.

"There are not too many women higher than her in the semiconductor industry, if any are," said Fred Zieber, president of Pathfinder Research (San Jose, Calif.). "She's gotten four promotions in four years, she's really moved ▶▶ **CONTINUED ON PAGE 132**

Possibly the most powerful woman in the semiconductor industry, King 'always aspired to be a CEO.'

SEPTEMBER 2002   VOL. 28, NO. 9

Electronic BUSINESS

THE BUSINESS MAGAZINE FOR THE ELECTRONICS INDUSTRY

Top 100 CMs
And Their
Fix-It Skills
page 50

Intel's Lablets:
Cost-Conscious
R&D
page 64

Hollywood's Plans
To Foil Copycats
page 72

MPEG-4:
Picture Imperfect?
page 80

First Lady

AMI Semiconductor's
Christine King: The first lady of
the semiconductor business
has a knack for customer care
page 40

Note

1   When we landed in Pocatello the pilots asked if they should
wait for us or return to San Francisco. Since we planned
to return the next day, Tom said they should just wait for
us. Of course, the next day was September 11th, and they
would end up stranded with us for almost a week.

Cow Cutting

I have shared a number of "new beginnings" in my career in this book, but my personal life has been marked by new beginnings as well. Unlike in my career where those beginnings typically were the result of "going around when I couldn't get through," new beginnings in my personal life were more often serendipitous and the result of being open to the wonder of the world and willing to explore and pursue emergent paths that struck my fancy.

When we moved to Idaho, I was excited to be living in the rugged West and ready to make good on my prediction to Sam Palmisano that I was going to be a cowgirl. I was 52 years old at the time and had not ridden a horse in more than 30 years, but not knowing how to do something has never dissuaded me from jumping in and getting started when it was something I wanted to do. But first, of course, I would need to get a horse.

I was in the San Francisco airport coming home from meeting with some AMI customers when I spied a *Cowboys & Indians* magazine, "The Premier Magazine of the West," in the newsstand. I picked it up and leafed through it on the flight home. On one of the glossy pages, I saw an advertisement with a picture of a woman sitting triumphantly on a beautiful horse in a gorgeous mountain setting. I thought to myself, *There you go. That's what I want to be.*

The next day, I called the number, and the woman in the picture answered. "Yes," she replied when I asked about horses. "We have a ranch in Oregon and sell horses to beginners just like you. We can sell you a 'Cadillac package,' with the horse, saddle, bridle, and a week of lessons with us in Oregon to get you up and riding." Well, that sounded just about perfect since I had never even put a Western saddle on a horse!

The next weekend, Jack and I drove to Richland, Oregon, and met Wil and Beverly Howe and walked around their ranch full of horses. I thought to myself, *Poor Jack! I'm always getting him into something—dairy farming, hiking to the highest point in all 50 states, and now I'm getting him into riding horses!* But I was hooked.

Looking around the ranch, it seemed to me that these people knew everything about horses and could teach me what I needed to know, or at least get me started. Beverly was a beautiful rider. Wil and Beverly recommended that we buy two horses—one for each of us—so we did. Sterling was a very spirited horse and a good match for Jack's personality, while Gus was quiet and more suited for me. We bought the horses but left them at the ranch until I could take vacation time a month later for our riding class.

As CEO, vacation time was rare and precious, so I wanted to get started on my riding lessons right away when we got to Oregon. As a result, I was a little annoyed on the first morning when Wil and Beverly had us sit around the fire and listen to non-horse-riding stories rather than saddling up and hitting the trail. I was ready to start riding! But we finally got to it, and I quickly discovered that it was harder than it looked and that I had to concentrate on not falling off. Jack was getting along great with Sterling, though, and after a week of instruction I had a little confidence and was excited to get Gus home and keep practicing.

I couldn't believe I owned a horse! I was enamored, and on the days I could go riding after work, it almost felt like I was going to meet a new boyfriend! But in short order, Gus recognized that I really didn't know what I was doing and decided he was going to do as he wished, despite my protestations. We would ride out into the field, and when we passed the trail back to the barn, he would throw his head up and start running in that direction. I couldn't figure out what was going on and how to get him to do what I wanted. I was starting to realize that Gus was not the ideal boyfriend I had thought. So, we made the long drive back to Oregon and Beverly with Gus in the horse trailer for remediation. Things seemed to get back on track, but a day or two after I got home again, Gus fell back into his old ways and would go running back to the barn when I wanted to ride into the field. This just wasn't working, and I was starting to lose my confidence. I also found that every time we galloped, I would start sliding off to one side. *Wow*, I thought to myself. *I have a lot to learn, and I might need a new horse!*

Fortunately, I discovered about that time that one of the AMI Semiconductor employees was an amateur horse trainer. Steve Larson worked in the failure analysis lab, so whenever I had a quick break for lunch, I would stroll down to the lab to get riding advice. I think my unannounced visits made the lab technicians nervous, but they soon got used to it.

On the weekends, I would put Gus in a trailer and go to Steve's ranch to improve my riding skills, and slowly but surely, things started getting better. In the spring, Steve told me that his mentor, a trainer named Patrick Wyse, would be coming through town to conduct a four-day clinic. He suggested I sign up, so I did. The clinic allowed each rider to bring two horses, so I brought Gus and got Jack to loan me Sterling. Pat was a tall and weathered cowboy from Montana and he had a way with horses *and* people. We were split up into groups according to ability and Pat sat in a judge's stand with a microphone watching us ride. While we galloped around the area showing our stuff, Pat would coach us in his loud but encouraging voice. It almost seemed like he was in my head, which made me so much braver, and I started feeling good galloping around the area and doing sliding stops and turns. For the first time, I started to feel like a real cowgirl!

That first clinic was so exciting. I was riding very well, but as I saw the other horses that my fellow riders had brought, and the horses Pat was riding, I realized Gus was a real dud. So, I started looking online for horses that were for sale, which led me to a young cowboy from Montana who was selling his ranch horse. Jack and I drove to Dillon, Montana, to check out the horse, and when the young man came to meet us, he could hardly talk because his jaw was wired shut—he had had a wreck when riding a bull at his high-school rodeo competition!

A thunderstorm was coming in, so we broke off our conversation and he jumped on his horse, Chex, to gallop out onto the Montana plain to gather some cows. It was quite a sight seeing this buckskin horse running across the wide-open field and jumping the ditches while lightning streaked out of the sky. "Yup," I said to Jack, "that is quite a horse; light years ahead of Gus." He seemed just right, so I purchased Chex as my next horse.

Chex and I became a favorite at the Pat Wyse clinics. On weekends I had free, we took our horse trailer all over the Northwest, from Idaho to Oregon and Washington State. By this time, I was itching to show off my horses and newfound riding skills and decided once again that some kind of competition would be a lot of fun. But what could I do?

As anyone who has watched the television series *Yellowstone* knows, there are three types of Western disciplines using performance horses—reining, cow horse, and cutting. Reining consists of galloping around on your horse and performing sliding stops and spins. Cow horse is when you ride along a fence next to a cow, cut the cow off with your horse, and then ride back down the fence in the other direction, before cutting the cow off again, which is dangerous because the horse's legs can get tangled up with the cow's legs, throwing and even killing the rider. Cutting is going head-to-head with a cow that you have "cut out" from the herd. I asked Pat which one was right for me. He said, "Reining is too boring, cow horse is dangerous—you could get killed—but cow cutting is just right." And so, I asked Pat to find me a cutting horse. He found Pepsi in Florida.

The thing about cow cutting is that once you cut the cow out of the herd, it wants to get back in the worst way. So, your horse ends up going head-to-head with the cow to keep it separated. The sport originated from cowboys and cowgirls having to separate a cow from a herd to give it medical attention or for some other reason. *Yellowstone* actually does a good job of displaying the sport in all its glory. The extra twist to the sport is that once you cut the cow from the herd, you have to drop the reins and stop using them to guide the horse! What a spectacular challenge—three minds in play: a rider, horse, and cow, all with different goals. And it is fast! It totally gets your adrenaline going!

So, I went to my first cutting show at a ranch outside Yellowstone National Park. Once again, I was trying to do something totally new, this time at the age of 60, and in a competition against men and women, young and old, many of whom had been cutting their entire lives. With my usual overconfidence, though, I drove to the show with Pepsi thinking I could kick some butt. When I arrived, however, it was a different story. I was scared! We were facing a huge herd of black cows, some of whom looked really wild! I didn't know how Pepsi or I would react. Would I fall off when Pepsi moved fast to catch the cow? As it turned out, I *did* almost fall off and ended up at the bottom of the class during the competition. It was a humiliating experience, and I am sure that all the experts were thinking, *Where did this crazy woman come from?* I was totally unprepared, and competition was much harder than I thought.

I drove home from the competition really humbled. But I wasn't going to give up! In my mind, it was once again a matter of having the right horse, finding the right trainer, and lining up all the needed allies. I kept at it and began to make progress.

Once I had successfully sold AMI Semiconductor, I was ready to make horses and cow cutting in Idaho my life. But then life intervened. Standard Microsystems (SMSC) in New York was looking for a new CEO, and the current CEO, Steve Bilodeau, thought I was the best person to take the reins (if you'll pardon the pun). I agreed to talk to him and made the mistake of telling Jack it sounded interesting. Jack had never bought into my dream of horse heaven in Idaho, and he thought I would be a great CEO for SMSC, even if it meant moving to Long Island. I shed many tears, crying, "I don't want to move to New York and leave my horses! And my new sport of cutting!" But I went to the interview, and once I was on the path toward running another company and realized the opportunity before me, I quickly got on board.

It took 14 tractor-trailer loads for us to move from Idaho, including the boat and the horses. While my main residence would be on Long Island, Jack thought it would be great to find a place where it was warmer, so we bought a house in Scottsdale, Arizona.

Well, I wasn't ready to give up on cow cutting, so I went on the National Cutting Horse Association website to see if there were any cutting trainers in New York, and there actually was one in Poughkeepsie. So, I loaded up the trailer and headed there with my horses. I always get a kick out of talking to my cutting friends in Arizona, California, and Texas about how I started this very Western sport in *New York*! My journey of cutting ended up taking me to competitions in Florida, Texas, California, Las Vegas, and everywhere in between. I learned how to assess a good horse, but more importantly, how to find a good program and a good trainer.

After I retired for a second time (by the way, it wouldn't be my last "retirement"!), Jack wanted to spend most of our time in Arizona. He kept asking me if there wasn't a place in Arizona where I could do my riding. I kept saying, "No, I need to ride in Texas!" When I really started looking into it, however, I learned there was a trainer, Mike Wood, and his partner, Roper Curtiss, who had a great cutting program. *And* they lived just 15 minutes from our Scottsdale house! So, we began the process of moving my horses one at a time to Arizona.

Now, 14 years since I started, I have won $330,000 in cutting competitions, and have finished in the top five amateur and non-pro riders in the world four times. And two of my horses have been world champions.[1] When I think back on how I started as a total and embarrassing disaster, I laugh, but as in my career, being persistent and finding the right allies enabled me to do something that I found thoroughly rewarding and allowed me to achieve great success—even in my seventies! It goes to show that it is never too late to embrace, learn, and enjoy a new path. Just put your ego aside and jump in!

Note

1   And along the way, my trainer, Mike Wood, became triple
     world champion and the top non-professional/amateur
     trainer in the world.

Afterword

Dear reader, thank you for sharing in my story. I hope that the lessons I learned along the way will help you write your very best story. Over the course of this book, I have introduced you to many of the wonderful people who walked with me for at least part of my journey. So, what ended up happening to them?

Lou Gerstner went on to write *Who Says Elephants Can't Dance?*, a bestselling book about his experiences turning around IBM. He continues to make huge contributions to society, and every time I hear him speak, I want to join whatever mission he is on.

John Kelly became the top technical head at IBM and is described as the father of Watson, the Artificial Intelligence computer system best known for competing against and beating humans on the TV show *Jeopardy*. He retired from IBM in January 2021 and will continue to play a significant role in maintaining and extending the US's leadership in semiconductor technology.

My first husband, **John**, kept on running. He battled alcohol and drugs his whole life, but always remained a gentle soul and songwriter. He passed away from cancer in 2021 and had not seen Eric since his fifth birthday.

My second husband, **Terry King**, continues to be a tinkerer in all things technological. He lives with his wife Mary Alice in the hills of Vermont.

My son **Eric** found a home for his many talents as an artist, animator, and songwriter. He possesses flawless character (and I'm not just saying that because I'm his mom!). He married Sarah and is the "Awesome Papa" of their beautiful daughter, Sydney.

My daughter **Megan** is a brilliant scientist and professor at Yale University. Like her mom, she is the consummate workaholic. Megan married her partner in science, Patrick, and is the mother of four wonderfully spirited children—Forrest, Lorelei, Hudson, and Adele.

And **Jack**, my best friend and husband, who became my lab partner more than 50 years ago, has been my partner in everything this glorious world has to offer to this day.

Thank you again for reading *Breaking Through the Silicon Ceiling*. If you have a few moments, please add your review of the book at your favorite online site for feedback. Also, please visit our website for news about upcoming events and recent blog posts: www.ChristineKing.com.

Sincerely,
Chris King

BUSINESS
BOOKS

Business Books

Business Books publishes practical guides
and insightful non-fiction for beginners and professionals.
Covering aspects from management skills, leadership and
organizational change to positive work environments, career
coaching and self-care for managers, our books are a valuable
addition to those working in the world of business.

15 Ways to Own Your Future
Take Control of Your Destiny in Business
and in Life Michael Khouri
A 15-point blueprint for creating better collaboration,
enjoyment, and success in business and in life.
Paperback: 978-1-78535-300-0 ebook: 978-1-78535-301-7

The Common Excuses of the Comfortable Compromiser
Understanding Why People Oppose
Your Great Idea Matt Crossman
Comfortable compromisers block the way of anyone trying to
change anything. This is your guide to their common excuses.
Paperback: 978-1-78099-595-3 ebook: 978-1-78099-596-0

The Failing Logic of Money
Duane Mullin
Money is wasteful and cruel, causes war, crime and
dysfunctional feudalism. Humankind needs happiness, peace
and abundance. So banish money and use technology and
knowledge to rid the world of war, crime and poverty.
Paperback: 978-1-84694-259-4 ebook: 978-1-84694-888-6

Mastering the Mommy Track
Juggling Career and Kids in Uncertain Times
Erin Flynn Jay
Mastering the Mommy Track tells the stories of everyday
working mothers, the challenges they
have faced, and lessons learned.
Paperback: 978-1-78099-123-8 ebook: 978-1-78099-124-5

Modern Day Selling
Unlocking Your Hidden Potential
Brian Barfield
Learn how to reconnect sales associates with customers
and unlock hidden sales potential.
Paperback: 978-1-78099-457-4 ebook: 978-1-78099-458-1

The Most Creative, Escape the Ordinary,
Excel at Public Speaking Book Ever
All the Help You Will Ever Need in Giving
a Speech Philip Theibert
The 'everything you need to give an outstanding speech'
book, complete with original material
written by a professional speechwriter.
Paperback: 978-1-78099-672-1 ebook: 978-1-78099-673-8

On Business And For Pleasure
A Self-Study Workbook for Advanced Business English
Michael Berman
This workbook includes enjoyable challenges and has been
designed to help students with the English they need for work.
Paperback: 978-1-84694-304-1

Small Change, Big Deal
Money as if People Mattered
Jennifer Kavanagh
Money is about relationships: between individuals and
between communities. Small is still beautiful, as peer
lending model, microcredit, shows.
Paperback: 978-1-78099-313-3 ebook: 978-1-78099-314-0

Readers of ebooks can buy or view any of these bestsellers by clicking on the live link in the title. Most titles are published in paperback and as an ebook. Paperbacks are available in traditional bookshops. Both print and ebook formats are available online.
Find more titles and sign up to our readers' newsletter at http://www.jhpbusiness-books.com/
Facebook: https://www.facebook.com/JHPNonFiction/
Twitter: @JHPNonFiction